HOPE
BENEATH
THE RUBBLE

Healing After Trauma

JENNIFER HAND

Hope Beneath the Rubble: Healing After Trauma

Print ISBN: 978-1-968889-02-9
Digital ISBN: 978-1-968889-03-6
Audio ISBN: 978-1-968889-04-3
LCCN: 2025916884

Cover and Interior Design by Nelly Murariu at PixBeeDesign.com
Manuscript Edits by Market Refined Media & Publishing

Printed in the United States of America
First Edition: September 2025

This book is dedicated to all the people
around the world who've allowed me
to stand alongside them on their holy
ground of suffering, among the rubble,
as we find hope together.

TABLE OF CONTENTS

Note from the Author   vii

Introduction   ix

Chapter 1: Earthquakes and Coffee   1

    Heart Work: When the Ground Shakes (and You Spill No Coffee)   9

Chapter 2: A New Normal After the Storms   13

    Heart Work: When the Storms Come (and the Toilet Paper Is Scarce)   22

Chapter 3: Needles and Normal Reactions to Trauma   27

    Heart Work: When Safety Feels Slippery and Side Effects Sneak Up   35

Chapter 4: Why Do I Feel Like I Cannot Get It Together?   41

    Heart Work: Permission to Limp (and Still Belong)   49

Chapter 5: Fight, Flight, Freeze, or Fawn   55

    Heart Work: Stress Responses and Other Superpowers in Disguise   68

Chapter 6: Is this Still Serving You?   73

   Heart Work: Stuck Isn't Forever: A Self-Check for
   the Fight, Flight, Freeze, or Fawned-Out   79

Chapter 7: What Your Brain and Body Can Do   83

   Heart Work: From Traffic Cop Chaos to Coffee Shop Calm   89

Chapter 8: Baby Steps, Breathwork, and Blasts of Cold   95

   Heart Work: When Serving No Longer Serves You   108

Chapter 9: Your Story Deserves to Breathe (Even If You're
Still in the Rubble)   115

   Heart Work: Tell It to Heal It   121

Chapter 10: Space to Hope Again   127

   Heart Work: Bricks, Blessings, and the Beginning of Hope 135

Acknowledgments   141

Appendix   142

Notes   145

About the Author   147

NOTE FROM THE AUTHOR

This book will encourage you throughout its chapters to find a mental health professional who can help you walk through your healing journey as you process trauma. You don't have to take this journey alone.

I also strongly encourage you to meet with your medical doctor if you're struggling with depression or anxiety. They can be an excellent resource for you as you navigate processing and healing from the deep wounds trauma can cause.

If at any point you feel like you're a danger to yourself or others and you live in the U.S., please call 911 or call or text the National Suicide Hotline at 988. If you're outside of the U.S., please seek out your country's emergency hotline number.

The names and situations of clients in this book have been changed to protect each client's privacy.

INTRODUCTION

Welcome to *Hope Beneath the Rubble*. I'm honored to have you here with me. This book has been years in the making, and I've written every sentence with a prayer on my heart for you.

When I received my master's degree in counseling *(two degrees in fact—what can I say, I love school, and frankly, I loved the social part of school!)* I had no idea the wild journey God would take me on.

I've been blessed to travel to over 50 countries and stand on the holy ground of suffering with people from all walks of life as I help them process their complex stories and their trauma. I also stand with them in their sufferings and hold onto hope for them.

In 2023, my sister's family and I traveled to the Dominican Republic to meet up with some friends who minister there. The work that Jamey and Elizabeth Davis and Jon Jon and Morgan Elicier are doing is amazing, and it was such a joy to witness their ministries. While there, I was asked to teach a trauma training to Haitian women living in the Dominican Republic.

I'd already seen firsthand the trauma many had experienced due to the violence and unrest in Haiti, so I was very honored to say yes to this request. As I taught about trauma and its effects, I wanted to have a resource to give them to take home. Something that would help them tangibly hold onto hope. That was the birth of the idea of writing this book. But can I be candid with you here? I didn't want to write this book. If you know anything about the Enneagram, I am an off-the-charts Enneagram 7, which means I want to have fun. I'm here for the party! Talking about feelings, trauma, and hard stuff—well, that's not fun. I am known for making readers laugh out loud with my writing.

I know what you're thinking. How did someone who just wants to have fun become a trauma counselor? That's a story for another time but trust me when I say, it's incredible where obedience to God will take you.

So, because of my love of laughter, a version of me feels the need to share a story with you about a time when I was in Turkey.

I'd been in the Middle East doing trauma care with refugees and had a layover at a Turkish airport. I was wearing a skirt that was a little too long but comfortable for the long days of traveling back home. Because I was in a hurry, I thought walking on the moving sidewalk would be a great and fast way to get through this massive airport.

It was a great idea until it wasn't.

I reached the end of the moving sidewalk, and my *slightly too-long* skirt got stuck. I walked off the end and kept moving forward, but my skirt did *not*. It got sucked into the moving sidewalk, and suddenly I was in the middle of this Middle Eastern airport in all my glory, unable to retrieve my skirt. I found myself laughing as I hurriedly looked for a bathroom to take cover in. *(It's ok, you can laugh too!)*

At that moment, I was vulnerable. Uncovered.

That's how it can feel when you talk about trauma. Vulnerable. Uncovered. All of the sudden, your breath is sucked out of you, and you wonder how you'll move forward without whatever was taken from you.

It's my prayer that this book helps you acknowledge the weight of what trauma has taken from you, while gently guiding and assisting you in moving forward after you've had time to take cover and heal.

What You Can Expect in the Pages to Come

We'll dive deeper into the definition of trauma, but simply put, *you experience trauma when you feel deeply unsafe physically, emotionally, relationally or spiritually.* Trauma impacts us all, but there is hope for healing and I'm here to help you experience it.

At the end of each chapter, there are "Heart Work" sections to guide you through each baby step of healing. Here you'll have space to journal, interact, process the ways trauma has impacted you, and discover how you can continue to find hope in your new normal. Don't feel pressure to do it at a particular time or to answer every question. Skip what doesn't serve you—it's a space for your own journey of healing.

As you seek healing from traumatic events, I pray this book offers support and encouragement. Healing can be found for you, my friend.

CHAPTER 1

EARTHQUAKES AND COFFEE

Superman. He was known to be able to leap tall buildings in a single bound. *(True confession: I had to Google which super-hero was known for that.)* I've never scaled a tall building, but I do have a skill I didn't know I possessed until it happened one evening in Turkey.

I discovered I could hold a cup of coffee and a cookie in one hand while jumping over a wall as a 7.6 earthquake rocked the earth. Not one drop of coffee spilled as I leaped the wall to get outside our building while the ground moved. I took a sip of coffee to steady my heart as the ground rolled, and looked around, preparing myself for the worst.

We were in an area packed very close together with houses. I will never forget the sounds of that evening. The sound of the earth rumbling as it moved. The sound of the buildings shifting. Things falling. But mostly the sounds of terrified people all around me. The sounds of already traumatized people full of panic, who were now being retraumatized before my very eyes.

It was February 2023, and I was in Turkey ministering on the holy ground of suffering. Turkey and Syria had recently experienced an earthquake which resulted in tens of thousands of deaths and complete devastation. Paired with my master's degree in counseling with an emphasis on trauma, my 'yes' to God has taken me around the world after natural disasters to provide trauma care in the aftermath of such crises.

I spent the week leading up to that second earthquake holding the hands and hearts of people who had lost so much. Many had lost family members. Most had lost their homes, workplaces, livelihoods, and sense of safety. I heard the horrific stories, smelled the lingering smell of death, and saw the buildings flattened to twisted concrete and glass rubble. And here I was, with these people, as they experienced the earth-shaking again.

At that moment, I wanted to be like Superman and leap tall buildings in a single bound. I wanted to be able to rescue people from their homes. I tried to hold their hearts until they felt safe again. Instead, I found myself leaping a wall, coffee in hand, realizing I was not Superman, but simply a woman watching the trauma of everything shaking around me.

When Everything Shakes

I imagine you picked up this book because your Earth has experienced shaking at some point. Maybe you haven't experienced a physical earthquake, but you have experienced something, or years of something, that has made everything feel unsteady, leaving devastation in its path.

Maybe you want to be like Superman but can barely even hold on to your coffee.

I want you to know that you're welcome here. I'm honored to stand or sit or kneel or crawl into this sacred space with you. In this space, you can admit that you've been through something traumatic, and you may not be sure how to rebuild from the rubble.

Sometimes, trauma happens in a moment; sometimes, it compounds over a lifetime. It can be easy to explain away trauma when we believe our trauma wasn't as bad as what our neighbor Sally experienced. You may call what you're feeling survivor's guilt or want to resist using the word trauma.

I want to stand here with you and do what I would if I were in your home after a natural disaster. People often ask me what I do or say as I help people process life-changing things like hurricanes, floods, fires, earthquakes, violent acts, etc.

Here's what I tell people:

The most important thing to do is to be physically present. To stand with people amid all their belongings outside of their freshly gutted house after a flood. To go to the hospital room and hold hands with the person who has just heard devastating news. To grab a bag and start picking up debris from a tornado. To show up and then hold space for their story.

So that's what we're going to do here. Let's both show up and hold space for your story.

Raise Your Hand

If I were speaking in a room full of people, what would your reaction be if I asked you to raise your hand if you had been through a trauma?

I imagine some hands would immediately go up because there is no doubt in your mind about your experience. Maybe you had a car accident, an assault, or a natural disaster. But perhaps you wonder if your relationship breakup or financial disaster counted? Maybe you would raise your hand because trauma seems to be trendy these days, and don't we all want to be trendy? Or perhaps you would be like me and think, how can I sneak out of the room and get a nice cup of strong coffee and avoid any trauma talk?

After the unexpected earthquake in Turkey, when I thought I was going to help in disaster relief, I came home forever changed. My literal and figurative earth had been shaken. I had not only seen and heard the worst stories in all my years of responding to natural disasters, but I'd also experienced the ground shaking myself.

When I got home, I realized I needed to take some space to heal, because the earth-shaking wasn't the only thing I needed to process.

During that time, I listened to *The Body Revelation: Physical and Spiritual Practices to Metabolize Pain, Banish Shame, and Connect to God with Your Whole Self* by Alisa Keeton. I heard her list some of the events in life that are considered trauma. *(As I am a trauma-trained therapist, I know these things for others, but it's too easy to forget for myself!)*

As I listened, I realized how many of these events had happened to me in the last year and a half of my own life. A car accident where I hydroplaned on an interstate, spun several times, hit someone head-on, and could have died—check. War—going to do trauma care in Ukraine when active missile attacks happened—check. Natural disasters—earthquake and tornado—check. And we can all add a collective going through a global pandemic trauma—check!

I realized I needed help processing these traumas, and I'm wondering if you might need help, too. I highly encourage you to find a trained counselor in your area. Ask your friends, pastor, and Google for recommendations. Reach out for help as you begin to process your trauma.

If you would raise your hand and say, "Wait, maybe I have been through some stuff!" I want to come up and stand beside you and remind you that you're not alone.

Biting Flies and Jellyfish

I recently was on a girls' trip to the beach. We were so excited to dig our toes in the sand. My friend purchased one of those fancy new beach tents that's more like a giant kite. I will say that I'm not the girl to figure out how to put these types of things together because it will end up a disaster.

We worked so hard to get our poles anchored in the sand. *(And by we, I just tried to do what they told me to do and often did it wrong!)* Things seemed to work until the wind shifted, and we no longer lazily sat under the tent in the sun. We were buried by the tent, unable to see the sun.

We got the tent set back up and were ready for round 2 when the plague of biting flies started. They were everywhere. And they weren't just flying around, annoying us; they were biting us. We quickly ran to the beautiful ocean water to escape them. Surely, if we jumped into the clear blue water and submerged ourselves, the flies couldn't find us there.

But guess what did find us? The Jellyfish. Apparently, there was a jellyfish plague happening as well. I have never seen so many jellyfish. They were everywhere, their tentacles ready to sting at any moment. We were now trying to avoid the stinging flies AND jellyfish.

Are you anxious reading this yet?

I relate this scenario for you because the effects of trauma can be like these jellyfish and biting flies.

You're trying to enjoy life, but the effects of your trauma just seem to keep coming at you. You may find yourself more anxious, unable to sleep at night. You may find yourself irritable. You may have intrusive flashbacks.

So, you try to outrun the effects of your trauma just like we ran to the ocean, but you realize there are other ways the lingering trauma is creating potential harm and disruption to you. It would be nice to ignore it, but that doesn't make it disappear.

I'm so excited to offer a gentle invitation to you for the steps to begin lessening the ways trauma impacts your daily life. It will always be part of you, but it doesn't always have to paralyze you. One day, there will be fewer jellyfish and flies, but only if you start facing your trauma now.

What about God?

Talking about trauma can bring up some big questions in our hearts about life. How can a good God allow bad things to happen? Where is God in these dark nights of the soul? Why didn't He stop me from having to experience _____?

As a trauma counselor, I've stood with, sat with, held hands with, and caught the tears of those who may be asking some of those heavy questions. I've held those questions in my own heart as I watched someone I loved suffer. And I've held those same questions, and many more, in my own heart, about my own suffering.

My least favorite class in graduate school was theodicy (theology) of trauma. It was a weekend-intensive class, and the only way I made it through was by thinking about ending each day with chips and salsa with friends. The class was full of heavy stuff to talk through and process. We spent more time in the book of Job than I ever wanted to.

This book won't be an intensive on the theology of trauma. Many people with more degrees and more smarts than me have written books for you on that. But I cannot write about hope beneath the rubble without incorporating the ultimate hope I've found: Jesus. I will never forget the first time I worked as a trauma counselor after a natural disaster.

For years, I'd served as a missionary in Nepal. I loved the people. I adored the culture, the language, the food, all the things. I lived there, made my home there, and left pieces of my heart there when I left.

Now I was stateside again. I was staying with a friend as she was grieving the death of her mom when I saw a news story that took my breath away and brought me to my knees.

A 7.8 earthquake had rocked Nepal. When I lived there, they consistently predicted the "big one." We had earthquake drills. We had an earthquake preparation box. But nothing can prepare you for when the earth shakes and everything changes.

The news showed pictures of the places that I loved—the people I loved—buried under rubble. I knew I had to get there. My freshly earned master's degree in counseling, my ability to speak Nepalese, and my love for the people led me to buy a plane ticket straight to Nepal.

There's always hope beneath any rubble. It's the hope of the cross.

After a long journey, I arrived in the village nearest the earthquake's epicenter. The villagers were gathered outside, clinging to each other along the side of a mountain in the middle of an aftershock. They were waiting for me as they heard I'd come to bring them hope. But this was my first encounter with such destruction, and I had no idea what hope I had to offer.

Church buildings are rare in Nepal, but there happened to be one in this village. They'd been having a service there when the earthquake occurred. Many were trapped inside the building, which was now a pile of rubble. I knelt beside the rubble, and something caught my attention.

It was the cross that had been on top of the church. It was broken and buried among the rubble, but you could still tell what it was. I sensed the Lord speaking to my heart, reminding me there's always hope beneath any rubble. It's the hope of the cross.

While the weight of questions you may have about God and your circumstances may be heavy right now, I want to encourage you with the hope of Jesus.

This isn't a place where I'm going to slap your heart with Romans 8:28 and tell you God is working all things for His glory and according to His purposes. I remember when my dad was in the hospital for thirty-one days fighting a battle with a rare leukemia, and people were telling me that verse over and over. I knew it but didn't want to hear it then. I just needed people to show up, bring a snack or barbeque sandwich, and let me know they were with me.

This book comes with an imaginary barbeque sandwich, chips, and a side of hope for you that Jesus is with you. However, please know you're welcome here regardless of where you are in your relationship with God.

Heart Work: When the Ground Shakes (and You Spill No Coffee)

Welcome to the part where we get intentional. We're not leaping over walls *(though, props to you if you are)*—we're taking one brave step toward healing. No superhero cape required.

Take a breath. Grab your favorite drink. And let's do a little *Heart Work*.

PS: If you aren't a word person, feel free to take some of these prompts to create a piece of artwork, a collage, or use whatever creative outlet works for YOU. Maybe you're a verbal processor and need to discuss this heart work with a friend instead. Feel free to be YOU!

1. Spill-Proof Strength

PROMPT: Recall a moment when "the ground shook" in your life—not literally, but emotionally, spiritually, or circumstantially. Write it out. Where were you? What happened? What did it shake in you?

_____

_____

_____

_____

_____

BONUS: Did you have a metaphorical "coffee and cookie" in hand—something you were trying to hold together while the world rocked?

2. The Soundtrack of Survival

PROMPT: In the story of your trauma, what are the sounds you remember—physical or emotional? (Sometimes the loudest "sounds" are silent: shame, confusion, exhaustion.)

Write a short paragraph (or list) of what you "heard" that season.

3. Raise Your Hand

REFLECTION: Imagine I'm in the room with you, passing out metaphorical coffee and barbeque sandwiches. If I asked, "Have you been through trauma?"—what would your body instinctively do?

Circle one:

- Hand up in the air waving for help.
- Half-raise, unsure.
- Hands down, but my heart is yelling "YES."
- I'm sneaking toward the door to avoid this question entirely.

Now ask yourself: *Why did I choose that response*? Let your honest answer surface, without judgment.

4. Vulnerable + Uncovered = Courageous

PROMPT: Write about a time you felt "skirt-less in the airport" or vulnerable. It might not be funny yet, but was there a moment you felt suddenly uncovered, seen, or exposed?

Then gently ask: What did that moment reveal about what I needed? What did I fear? What did I believe?

_____

_____

_____

_____

5. Hope in the Rubble

REFLECTION + VISUALIZATION: Close your eyes briefly _(after you read this part, of course)_. Picture a place in your life that feels buried. Rubble everywhere. Messy. Confusing. Then imagine the cross—maybe cracked, dusty, but unmistakably there—right in the middle of it.

Now open your eyes and write this sentence:

"Hope beneath my rubble looks like _____."
Write what hope looks like to you even if it feels unsure, shaky, or unfinished.

_____

_____

_____

_____

6. Speak This Over Yourself

Say this out loud. Yes, out loud. (If you're in public, whisper it into your coffee cup.)

"My story matters, even if I don't know how to tell it yet.

My pain is real, even if someone else had it 'worse.'

My healing is possible, even if I can't see it yet.

And I don't have to do it alone."

That's enough brave for today. You did it. You showed up.

Take a deep breath. Maybe grab a snack. *(Preferably one without jellyfish or biting flies.)*

Next chapter? Let's keep showing up together.

CHAPTER 2

A NEW NORMAL AFTER THE STORMS

Raise your hand if you remember what a wild year 2020 was.

Do you find yourself having a physical reaction even just thinking about it? Recently, my sister and I were reminiscing about how excited we were when we were able to find our mom's favorite kind of toilet paper for her birthday gift. We had to climb two shelves to reach it because it was hidden at the very top. *(If you're wondering, we grew up with the fancy name-brand toilet paper with lotion. Now that I'm a grown-up and buy my toilet paper on my budget, I buy the one-ply, barely-there stuff for myself.)*

On Easter Sunday evening of 2020, my small group and I played a game on Zoom. It had been the strangest Easter Sunday I could remember. Church had been online. We weren't sure it would be safe to be with my parents, so we met them outside and didn't even hug them *(and we're a big-time hugging family)!* We even sanitized the grocery bags in which we brought the Easter eggs.

That night, while we were hanging out together via Zoom, our phones alerted us there was a storm warning for that evening. We didn't think much about it, continuing to laugh and chat. We finished the Zoom call at around 10:30, just as the thunder started to rumble. No big deal, just a simple spring thunderstorm.

I was on Facebook and saw the local weatherman go live, so I clicked more out of boredom than anything else. They were also treating this like a simple spring thunderstorm, even joking with the live audience as they showed the radar on the screen.

Suddenly, there was an abrupt change in the meteorologist's voice. I can still vividly remember one of them beginning to cry. They called out a street name and, in hurried, raised voices, said, "If you are on or near this street, take cover now. A tornado has formed and is about to touch down!"

I was on that street.

I quickly ran outside and grabbed my upstairs neighbor to bring her and her daughter into the corner of my semi-underground room. She screamed as I prayed Psalm 91:1–6 hovering in the darkness of my bedroom corner . . .

He who dwells in the shelter of the Most High
will abide in the shadow of the Almighty.
I will say to the Lord, "My refuge and my fortress,
my God, in whom I trust."
For he will deliver you from the snare of the fowler
and from the deadly pestilence.
He will cover you with his pinions,
and under his wings you will find refuge;
his faithfulness is a shield and buckler.
You will not fear the terror of the night,
nor the arrow that flies by day,
nor the pestilence that stalks in darkness,
nor the destruction that wastes at noonday.

Psalm 91:1–6

The whole house seemed like it would explode in one moment. Sounds as those of a train rushing by, the crackling of a tree falling on the bedroom upstairs, the water dripping through the ceiling landing on my head all filled the air.

The tornado had hovered over our house but didn't touch down.

Everything Looks Different

That night was filled with neighbors helping neighbors, trying to make sense of what had just happened. The next day, as someone who'd traveled the world to provide trauma care to those impacted by natural disasters, I found the disaster had come to my home, to the streets I'd grown up around, to the people I knew and loved.

I drove to the area of town where the EF3 tornado had touched down, and I couldn't even find my way around because everything looked different. The path of destruction carved through our town made the streets and areas unrecognizable. It was hard to navigate the roads with all the rubble littered about.

One neighbor found some of their belongings three streets over, in a tree. Another was wandering around looking for their pet that had flown through the air. Other people had a dazed look in their eyes over what had just happened. Remember, this horrific event took place during the height of the pandemic confusion, so we weren't even sure how we were supposed to—or even allowed to—interact with people.

In the following months, I spent every day in those streets, helping people walk through their trauma, making sure they had a safe place to tell their stories. Often, as we talked, we also sorted through their remaining belongings, trying to see what could be kept and what had to go. Their treasures often had to be placed in piles to be hauled away as junk.

Some had only a few walls of their home remaining. Some had only a few boards or the foundation of their homes remaining. Some had their home with no belongings remaining.

But they all had one question in common.

I've been asked this same question after responding to war victims in the Middle East and Ukraine and earthquake victims in Ecuador, Nepal, or Turkey; cyclone victims in Mozambique; hurricane victims in Texas and Florida; flood Victims in Louisiana. It may have been asked in different languages under different circumstances, but it was still the same question.

"Will life ever feel and look normal again?"

This is the same question I heard in the counseling room where I saw clients. They may have dealt with years of childhood trauma, divorce, loss of a loved one, grief over a child who was estranged, teenagers who felt lost in the crowd, anxiety, depression, or financial troubles.

The question people were asking is, *"Will life ever feel and look normal again?"*

Rebuilding is Possible

The healing journey often starts with the question, "Will I ever feel normal again?"

As the months passed after the April tornado hit my hometown, I noticed the questions slowly changed for the residents I continued to meet with. As they dealt with insurance companies *(talk about trauma)* and tried to figure out FEMA paperwork, they were beginning to ask what rebuilding looks like.

I want to encourage you: rebuilding is possible.

You may want to take a deep breath and re-read that statement. *(Breathing is a great way to decrease the effects of trauma, so go ahead and just do it! Take a deep breath.)* Now, let's re-read that statement again.

> Rebuilding
> is possible.

Rebuilding is possible.

You may not feel like you can hold on to this hope right now, and that's okay. If that's you, I encourage you to find someone who can hold hope for you. Find a friend, a counselor, a teacher, or a mentor who can walk this journey with you, encouraging you to know that you're not alone, and hoping for you when finding hope may seem impossible to you.

As you begin to hold on to hope, the question may shift from, "Will I ever feel normal again?" to, "What will rebuilding my life after experiencing trauma look like? What is my new normal?" Finding a *new* normal can feel scary, overwhelming, and exhausting. Remember, "Sometimes faith means looking past the landscape of destruction around us to the restoration God has promised on the horizon."[1]

I like to use the acrostic RUBBLE as I help individuals move forward to find hope beneath the rubble of trauma. When I first started teaching about trauma using this acrostic, I was leading trauma debriefings for those who'd experienced a life-changing earthquake as we gathered, literally, among the ruins and rubble. I realized as I looked at the building rubble and the people around it that these people were desperate to know the rebuilding of their lives would be possible. But I saw they needed tools to help them find the steps to possibility and healing. These tools included understanding the trauma they'd gone through by looking at how one can use the brain and body to understand triggers and processes, and how leaning on others for encouragement and support can slowly lend itself to experiences of fresh hope.

RUBBLE

Rebuilding is Possible

Understand Trauma and Its Effects

Brain

Body

Leaning into Others and how to ask for help

Experience Hope

Hope kept them alive.

This acrostic begins and ends with hope. I've talked with several earthquake victims in other countries who spent hours or days buried underneath actual rubble. I asked them what kept them alive, buried underneath that rubble.

All of them had the same response: hope. *Hope kept them alive.*

When a Big Scientific Word Can Give You Hope

I want to give you a big scientific word that can provide hope that rebuilding after trauma is possible.

Neuroplasticity!

The American Psychological Association Dictionary of Psychology defines neuroplasticity as follows: "the ability of the nervous system to change in response to experience or environmental stimulation."[2]

What this means for you is that you *are not* stuck forever. Your nervous system, your brain, and your responses can change. Yes, trauma can cause your brain to feel stuck in the past. When you have experienced trauma, it can create a fixed network in your brain that's isolated from other parts of your brain *(we will dive deeper into the brain in the middle section of the book)*, making you feel stuck and resistant to change. However, neuroplasticity means your brain can learn new patterns.[3]

Have you ever been in your car, driving on such a familiar route that you zone out and don't even realize it? Suddenly, you find yourself home from the grocery store with your favorite chocolate chip cookies and the coffee you needed to survive the next morning, and you don't even know how you got there. You were on autopilot. Our brains can get stuck on autopilot after trauma, but neuroplasticity reminds us that we can find new, healthier pathways. "The importance of neuroplasticity can't be overstated: It means that it is possible to change dysfunctional patterns of thinking and behaving and to develop new mindsets, new memories, new skills, and new abilities."[4]

I love what Wendy Blight says in her book *Rest for Your Soul*. "God, our wise and all-knowing Creator, designed the human brain to adapt to physical and emotional trauma. God created our brains in such a way that each of us can literally change the brain's physical structure by helping it make new connections through new activities and experiences. Some of the changes will strengthen current connections and eliminate others. Some can even create new neural connects, called sprouting."[5]

Where Are You?

To work the gift of neuroplasticity in your brain, you must ask where you are in your journey. Are you a little further from the trauma and just need to tell your story so that you don't feel as alone? Are you triggered by experiences seemingly unrelated to the actual traumatic event even many years after that event? If you were standing among the rubble after an actual natural disaster, you would be looking around to see what pieces you could grab. You'd be looking for what was salvageable. You would begin to sort piles of keep, destroyed, needs to be gutted out, etc.

What pieces do you see around you as you think about your life? What things do you want to keep/salvage? What would you like to see destroyed? What may need some gutting?

After you think about where you are, think about where you want to be.

What would rebuilding your life after experiencing trauma look like to you? Begin to dream about your new normal as we find space to hope again.

Healing for Different Types of Traumas

It can be helpful to understand the different types of traumas as you begin your journey to healing. Francine Shapiro, Ph.D., developed EMDR, a widely used therapy technique to help in recovery from trauma. He categorizes trauma into two different types.

Big "T" trauma includes events that a person perceives as life-threatening: combat, crimes such as rape, kidnapping, assault, natural disasters and accidents.[6] He writes, "Small "t" trauma, on the other hand, occurs in the innocuous but upsetting adverse experiences that daily life sends our way. It can result in some of the same feelings as big "T" trauma and have far-reaching consequences."[7]

Some of you have had a significant experience that you have no doubt is a big "T" trauma. You know you went through that natural disaster, car accident, or assault. But I imagine many of you may even feel slightly guilty or unworthy to say difficult things in your story equate to trauma. It can be so easy to play the comparison game with trauma. I look at someone else's story and then tell myself that my own experience wasn't THAT bad, so how can I say I need help?

I encourage you not to look at Sally's story of losing her whole family in a house fire and then think that your years in an emotionally abusive relationship aren't the same. They may be different circumstances, but both require healing. They don't need to be compared to the other.

In her book *Try Softer*, Aundi Kolber describes big "T" trauma like a person with a deep knife wound who needs immediate emergency room care, and little "t" trauma like a person with 1000 paper cuts who is less likely to get care, and then the hand eventually gets infected. She reminds us, "Whether the trauma is big or little, people find great relief when they receive validation that their wounds need care."[8]

Big "T" or little "t," your wounds need care. And there is hope for healing from wounds of trauma. Whether it's big "T" or little "t", you can hope and work toward a new normal.

Heart Work: When the Storms Come (and the Toilet Paper Is Scarce)

Will life ever feel normal again?

Let's take a few brave steps toward that answer. And remember, if you're less into words and express yourself another way, feel free to drawing, paint, cut out pictures and words from a magazine and make a collage—whatever helps you process!

1. Where Were You When the Storm Hit?

PROMPT: What's a "storm" you've lived through?

Describe:

- Where were you?
- What were you doing?
- Who showed up for you?
- What did you feel?

2. Normal–ish?

REFLECTION: When you read or hear the word "normal," what emotions rise in you?

Circle any that apply or add your own:

- Longing
- Grief
- Confusion
- Frustration
- Hope
- Bitterness
- "LOL, what even is normal?"

Then finish this sentence:

Right now, my version of "normal" looks like _____

_____ .

3. What Needs Gutting?

Just like those sorting piles after the tornado—keep / trash / gut / maybe salvage— trauma often leaves us with emotional and spiritual debris to sort through.

Make four columns and fill in a few honest answers:

Keep (these still serve me)	Trash (no longer needed)	Gut (this needs healing)	Maybe Salvage (let's revisit later)
my faith	pretending I'm fine	my fear of the future	that relationship I'm not sure about

4. A Big Word + Big Hope

Neuroplasticity. It's not just fun to say—it means you're not stuck.

Write a sentence like this:
A pattern I'd love to change in my brain is _____.

Then another:
A new pathway I'd love to build is _____.

For example: A pattern I'd love to change in my brain is always feeling like everything is an emergency. A new pathway I'd love to build is: Slow down, breathe, this may not be an emergency situation.

This is your first gentle brick in the rebuilding process.

5. Permission to Be Human

Whether you've been through a big "T" trauma or 10,000 little "t" traumas that left you cut up and tired . . .

Say this out loud: "My wounds are valid. My pain deserves care. I don't need a trauma comparison chart to start healing."

As a constant reminder for you, write that on a sticky note. Or your mirror. Or your toilet paper roll. Whatever and wherever works. Just keep it handy so that you're able to remind yourself often of these truths.

6. Shadow of the Almighty

Go back to the beginning of this chapter and slowly reread Psalm 91 then write it out in the space below.

Next, in a quiet moment, complete this sentence:

Under His wings, I want to rest from _____ .

You're doing the work. You're showing up. You might be just a little wobbly and tired—but you're here. And that counts.

Take a breath. Hydrate. Stretch. Find a little corner of hope to curl up in today.

I'll meet you in the next chapter.

CHAPTER 3

NEEDLES AND NORMAL REACTIONS TO TRAUMA

I hate needles. I didn't even get the shots they recommended when I was moving to Nepal because I didn't want to do the whole needle thing. So, you know I was feeling a little bit desperate when I returned from experiencing the earthquake in Turkey and signed myself up for acupuncture.

My equilibrium was off because of the earthquake, and I found myself dizzy and struggling with balance. My friend had spoken highly of her acupuncture experience. She was like those Instagram ads that come and tell you that you need something you didn't even know you needed. *(Please tell me I'm not alone and that you've bought something from an Instagram ad you didn't even know you needed, like a lip plumper that numbs your lips!)*

I found myself sweating in the parking lot before I even opened the door to go into the office. Why did I sign up to be poked with tiny needles? Once inside, I found they had the excellent smells of a massage therapy office, the soft music playing, and the lights dimmed, but it did nothing to calm my anxiety.

I giggled as I remembered another time, signing up for a coffee massage without reading the fine print of what I was in for.

I had imagined I'd be sipping coffee while getting a massage. But no! Little did I know they'd vigorously scrub all the skin off my body with a coffee rub, pour warm water over it, wrap me in Saran wrap, and leave me there to brew.

There was no coffee sipping here either. Just me about to go into a room with a lady who was going to poke me with needles.

My acupuncturist was great. She asked a ton of questions and made me feel super comfortable. I could tell she knew her stuff, and she thought she could help. So, we proceed with the appointment. I laid face down, because she said that was best. She did a fantastic job poking me with lots of needles in what she said were just the right places. The bonus prize was the massage at the end, but no coffee was included.

The one session seemed to help, so I decided to do it again because, for it to be most effective, they said I needed to come consistently for the next few weeks. My own acupuncturist *(words I never thought I'd say)* couldn't fit me in the next week, so I scheduled with a different gal.

I walked in just as nervously, even though I'd experienced this before. And my nerves quickly heightened as she started talking all this medical jargon. She clearly knew her stuff, but I felt my blood pressure rise. Then she told me she was going to bleed my ear.

Talk about making my palms sweaty. I didn't even know what she meant, but ear-bleeding sounded intense. Don't get me wrong, she was so sweet and brilliant, but I was only getting more nervous by the minute. And then she asked to do the acupuncture face-up.

I lay there trying to be okay but still felt increasingly anxious. She noticed as my body began pouring sweat, and I felt like I was going to faint. Not only was she working on the points to help with dizziness, but she was also putting needles in my ear to help with PTSD, and I wasn't sure at what exact point the "bleeding of the ear" was going to happen.

We both concluded she needed to stop, or I might pass out. She asked if she could leave the needles in that were already in place and let me lie there for about twenty minutes. I said yes.

After she left, the strangest thing happened. Tears kept leaking down my face. I'm not typically a crier, so I was surprised by this. I cannot explain why this was happening, but there I was, crying on the acupuncture table.

When she returned to the room, she explained that my body was looking for a sense of safety. She reminded me that the earthquake made me feel unsafe, and now, being here face up without the feeling of support from the table, I was feeling unsafe again.

That perfectly described what was happening to my body: sweaty palms, feeling faint, etc.

If you've experienced any trauma, whether an acute traumatic event or years of complex childhood trauma, your body is looking for a sense of safety.

Aundi Kolber, therapist and author of *Strong Like Water*, had a quote on Instagram that I find very helpful in defining trauma. "Trauma happens when we experience a profound rupture in safety (related to emotions/relationships/faith/health/reality, etc.) and the repair doesn't match the wound."[9]

One of the ways we help re-establish a sense of safety for those who have walked through the trauma is by normalizing their response to the event. I want to normalize the trauma response for you.

I've counseled many who feel guilty or confused by their emotional reactions after a traumatic event. Why can they not seem to be present with their family? Why do they find themselves dissociating when they're with them? They may describe

feeling numb or in a fog. They experience tiredness and confusion they cannot get over. Someone asked me why they kept
putting their keys in the refrigerator after they put their groceries
away. It's essential to know the immediate and delayed effects
of trauma so that you can know you're responding to abnormal
circumstances in a normal way.

That One Time in an Airplane

I was recently on an airplane for eight hours, traveling to London.
I was chaperoning for our youth mission trip to Scotland. Several
of our youth were on a plane for the very first time. This happened
to be about my five hundredth time. I have flown in everything
from big planes to aircraft so small that you sit with the pilot.
I must admit, though, this time I got nervous before we even
boarded the plane. We sat chatting in the Atlanta airport when
they told us over the speaker the pilot shared that our flight was
going to be turbulent.

"Play it cool, Jenn," I told myself. I wanted to act okay. However,
the truth is, after being in the earthquake, I struggle with flight
turbulence. Turbulence mimics the feeling of the earthshaking.
If you're inside a building during an earthquake, you must leave
the building as quickly as possible for your safety. When you're
on a plane, there's no getting out.

We boarded the plane. The flight took off and things were
going okay until, suddenly, they were not. *(If you already fear
airplanes, you may want to skip this section.)* The flight attendants had their drink carts and were passing out drinks when
suddenly it felt like the plane was dropping out of the air.

It was so extreme that everyone not in their seatbelt went
flying. The drink cart flew up. The flight attendants hit the ground
and assumed what looked like the crash position to me.

My leg flew up over the seat in front of me. I gripped the seat with both hands and tried to remind myself to breathe. My brain and body instantly responded. My brain told me I was in an earthquake and needed to escape. My body got the signal from my brain that there was danger, so it began to shake. Vigorously.

I told myself to breathe.

I knew the plane would probably not crash, but it was hard to connect with that reality. My body went into hyperarousal mode. This can be one of the responses to trauma. You become hyperaware and vigilant, waiting for the next danger. My legs didn't stop shaking for a few hours, and I was on the edge of my seat for the rest of the flight. It helped me to know that these reactions were normal physical and emotional reactions, which is why I want you to know that we do feel the effects of past trauma.

Immediate Reactions to Trauma

Jessie was attacked by a dog and found herself physically shaking afterwards, even days after the attack. Shaking can be a common immediate physical reaction to trauma.

Seth watched his friend being badly injured on the job site. He generally loves himself a big dinner—food is his love language. But since the accident, he has completely lost his appetite and feels nauseous all the time. We often feel the immediate effects of trauma in our gut.

Casey had to go to the school nurse because her heart rate was so high. She had been taken out of her parents' home the day before because domestic violence had gotten so bad. High heart rates and rapid breathing are another physical reaction to trauma.

You may experience sleeplessness or startled responses to sounds or other stimuli. Do you find yourself highly exhausted, feeling like your feet are made of lead? Is it overwhelming to try to put one foot in front of the other? Do you feel like your brain is in a fog? Are you numb, detached, and having difficulty concentrating?

You may want to withdraw from others. It can be challenging to be around people if they haven't experienced the trauma you've walked through. Their lives have gone on while yours has potentially changed forever.

These are all immediate effects of trauma. *(Why do I feel like I am doing a medical commercial for drug side effects? You know, the kind where they tell you all the benefits of the medicine and then go on for what feels like minutes talking about the side effects.)*

I was talking with Terrance as we stood outside her home, which had been destroyed by Hurricane Harvey. She told me her emotions felt out of control. One minute, she felt guilty for surviving with what she had. Another minute, she felt extreme anger followed by profound sadness. As her neighbor and I stood with her outside their homes amongst all the ruined possessions, they discussed how despite all those emotions, they still experienced hope. They had hope that they would rebuild, hope that they would survive this tragedy and only come out stronger.

This wide range of big feelings is a very natural response to trauma.

After my car accident, I had difficulty remembering things I needed to do that week. My thoughts were also distorted. I felt such guilt and shame for having injured someone in the accident that my distorted thinking led me to feel like I should never drive again, so I could never hurt someone again.

If you're a praying person, after a traumatic event, you may find yourself praying more, or you might find yourself praying less. It's okay if God feels like your safe place now, and it's okay if He does not. In the Psalms, you'll find all kinds of emotions. The highs and the lows, the desperation, the praise. This pattern in Scripture reminds me that we can pour out our hearts in prayer with all our emotions. But there are times when we cannot pray or even want to pray.

There was a time during my dad's thirty-one day hospital stay for leukemia that I didn't want to pray. I couldn't pray. A friend *(who brought a barbeque sandwich, of course!)* reminded me of this verse:

> "For we do not know what to pray for as we ought, but the Spirit himself intercedes for us with groanings too deep for words."
>
> Romans 8:26

If you think about it, Jesus knew He'd experience the trauma of the cross and the shameful, brutal death it would bring. And He knew He was about to be betrayed by one of his closest friends. In the Garden of Gethsemane, He prayed so hard that He sweated drops of blood. That was an immediate physical response to trauma. I pray that none of you have had to experience sweating drops of blood.

If you're experiencing any of these effects from trauma, I pray that reading the list makes you feel less crazy. Even if you cannot, at times, seem to remember your own name!

Delayed Effects of Trauma

It is normal to want to put a timeline on healing. But as we just discussed, trauma does have a ripple effect that can last long after the traumatic event.

Tara came to me for counseling after the sudden loss of her mother. Her mother had a heart attack while Tara was driving in the car with her, and Tara had to perform CPR until the medics came. By then, it was too late. Tara found herself wondering why, almost a year later, she was still struggling with grief. She also struggled with the fear that she would again dramatically lose someone else she loved.

Part of her struggle was that she felt she should be over the grief and feelings of fear by now. Maybe you think that way as well. You feel it's been too long and want to be passed this "stage" already. Surely, we're still not expected to deal with this.

It is so important to remember that the effects we feel on our physical body, our emotions, and relationships can be delayed and experienced long after the trauma. Mood swings, irritability, and anxiety are signs that our body and soul are still trying to process the trauma.

These are normal reactions to abnormal circumstances, and in the following chapters, we'll discuss how the brain and body work together after trauma and how you can use the tools presented to help lessen the effects of the trauma.

Heart Work: When Safety Feels Slippery and Side Effects Sneak Up

This chapter covered a lot: Acupuncture tears, plane turbulence, and that awkward coffee massage. But beneath it all was a more profound truth:

> Trauma affects our body. Our brain. Our ability to feel safe. And—here's the clincher—you're not broken. You're human.

Let's normalize some things together, shall we?

1. What's Your "Needle"?

PROMPT: What seems small to others, but makes your body go, "Nope!" even now?

It might be:

- A loud sound
- A certain smell
- A crowded room
- Being still
- Being touched
- Being out of control (aka turbulence city)

Write it out. Try starting with:

"One thing that feels hard for me since what happened is
_____."

For example: Since the accident, I have a hard time when I hear and see rain on the road.

2. Faceup, Facedown, or Nowhere Near the Table?

My acupuncturist told me I felt unsafe lying face-up because I lacked the physical support of the table. It struck me as such a powerful metaphor.

REFLECTION: When do you feel "face-up"—exposed, unsupported, or on edge?

When do you feel "face-down"—more secure, grounded, or safe?

What could help you build more "table support" daily?

For example: Do you feel "face-up" when you're in a crowded area with loud noises? Do you feel "face-down" when you're with your friend group at a coffee shop?

3. When the Plane Drops

Think about a moment when your brain and body went into panic mode—maybe recently, maybe years ago. It doesn't have to be a "big" event.

What happened?
How did your body respond?
What did you *wish* someone had said or done in that moment?

Write a few sentences starting with:

"I didn't feel safe when _____."

"What I needed was _____."

For example, I didn't feel safe when I was at the family Thanksgiving table. What I needed was someone there who I could share with that I needed a moment to recover from panic.

_____

_____

_____

_____

4. Side Effects May Include . . .

Trauma reactions are like those commercials listing 800 side effects. *You may experience sweaty palms, memory loss, emotional outbursts, sudden craving for casseroles . . .*

PROMPT: List three "side effects" you've noticed in yourself—physical, emotional, mental, or spiritual—that surprised you.

Then write beside each one:

🌿 "This is a normal reaction to an abnormal situation."

Example:

- 🌿 I forget people's names → normal response to stress
- 🌿 I avoid talking to people → normal reaction to overwhelm
- 🌿 I cry at random dog commercials → yep, also normal

- 🌿 _____ → _____
- 🌿 _____ → _____
- 🌿 _____ → _____

5. The Lie vs. The Truth

Sometimes trauma tells us lies like:

- 🌿 "I should be over this by now."
- 🌿 "I'm too sensitive."
- 🌿 "Other people have it worse."
- 🌿 "I must be going crazy."

PROMPT: Write one lie that trauma whispers to you. Then speak the truth to it.

Like this:

Lie: "I should be doing better."
Truth: "Healing isn't linear, and I'm doing my best."

The Lie vs. The Truth

LIE	TRUTH
I should be doing better.	_Healing isn't linear, and I'm doing my best._

6. When You Can't Pray

You're not alone if prayer feels hard, awkward, painful, or quiet. We've all had our Romans 8:26 moments.

PROMPT: Finish this sentence: "Right now, I wish I could tell God _____."

Then finish another: "If I could feel one thing from God right now, it would be _____."

And if words don't come? That's okay too. He hears groans, sighs, and silence.

7. Post-It Theology

Write one sentence of comfort or truth you want to carry this week. Something to stick on your mirror, fridge, or laptop's inside. Something like:

"It's okay to be not okay yet."

"My body is not betraying me—it's protecting me."

"Healing is happening, even if I can't see it."

You're not behind. You're rebuilding.

Take a deep breath.

Pour yourself that coffee. Or grab that cookie.

You've done Heart Work today. And that's a huge deal.

WHY DO I FEEL LIKE I CANNOT GET IT TOGETHER?

I tend to be a procrastinator, but I also like to set goals. I set a specific goal for finishing this book but, let me be honest, that doesn't mean I didn't find ways to procrastinate the writing of it.

I set a goal to write the entirety of Chapter 4 within a few hour blocks of time, but I also decided that afterwards I needed to go on a walk, even though it was about twenty degrees outside. It had been a snowy week here in our small town in Tennessee. We got about 4 inches of snow on a Friday, and schools were still out on this particular day, a Tuesday, because that's how we roll here in the south. *(I can picture my friends who live in cold places rolling their eyes!)*

I enjoyed my cold procrastination walk while using the Marco Polo video chat with my dear friend Deb. *(If you're unfamiliar with Marco Polo, it's an app that allows you to send video messages to friends. You can also tell when they are watching live, and Deb happened to be watching live.)*

I was busy telling her all about how I was starting to dive into writing chapter four when suddenly I was hitting the ground. My feet went out from under me, my bottom hit the ground hard, but I somehow managed to keep the phone in my hand. My poor friend Deb got quite the angle as she watched this happen live.

I'd slipped on some black ice. The pavement looked fine to me, until I found myself on the ground! I got back up, and laughed, knowing I'd scraped my knee, was bleeding, and would have a big bruise—but that I would be okay. I was saying to her, "Sorry you had to see that," when suddenly I was on the ground again. I slipped on more black ice.

Down I went again! As I got up, I told poor Deb again, "Sorry you had to see that!" I laughed to deflect the fact that I was in pain, and I decided to end my winter writing procrastination walk quickly.

I didn't recognize the black ice. I had no idea I was about to slip and fall. I didn't have time to brace myself because I didn't know the impact I would experience.

My friend Deb is from Minnesota. They deal with snow, ice, and cold all the time so they're much more prepared than we are. They know what to look for and do, and how to handle this kind of extreme weather. Deb began to tell me how black ice works and how tricky it is because even if everything around looks melted, there could be a slippery spot you cannot see that didn't melt due to shade, an exhaust pipe from a car, or all manner of different things.

Why am I telling you this procrastination story? It was the perfect way to explain how a trauma trigger works. You may be going about your everyday life and suddenly have a big reaction to an event. It can be an emotional reaction, a physical reaction, or a combination of both.

Just like black ice, you may not see it coming, and it completely interrupts what you're doing. When you experience a trauma trigger, you can feel like you fell flat on your back, or the wind was knocked out of you. Over and over, I've had people who have experienced trauma say to me, "Why can't I just get over it, get it together, respond normally? Why do certain things seem to impact me out of nowhere?" I've asked myself these same questions at times. That's why I want us to have this information so that we feel empowered to know what is normal and how to recognize trauma triggers and their effects.

The American Psychological Association defines a trauma trigger as a "stimulus that elicits a reaction. For example, an event could be a trigger for a memory of a past experience and an accompanying state of emotional arousal."[10]

Sometimes a trigger can make it feel like you are experiencing a past event in the present. For example, someone who's had relational trauma or physical trauma, even if they've been out of that relationship for years, can be triggered by raised voices. They can have an immediate, unwelcome physical or emotional response. Sights, sounds, places, dates, and familiar situations can trigger you.

Our brains are designed to keep us safe. They are triggered into fight, flight, freeze, or fawn survival mode when they sense something unsafe.

"When you encounter a trigger, memories and thoughts associated with the trauma come back without warning. You cannot stop the intrusive thoughts, and in response, you feel a turn in your emotions and begin to react.

A trigger might make you feel helpless, panicked, unsafe, and overwhelmed with emotion. You might feel the same things that you felt at the time of the trauma, as though you were reliving the event."[11]

While working on my counseling degrees, we often used role-playing in class. One of us would pretend to be the client, and one would be the counselor. Role-playing in front of a class was always a way to make me hope my deodorant worked for my sweaty armpits. There was something very difficult about entering into someone's pain *(even if it was pretend)* and offering healing and hope while on display in front of the class.

Let's do a little role play right now. Pretend I'm your counselor. You sit down in my cozy office. I hold a coffee cup in my hand, and you start sharing about your experience that week.

You had come upon an automobile accident that week on your drive to work. You thought you should be over it by now, because it was ten years ago when you came upon the accident that took the life of your mother. But this new car accident triggered you. Your heart started to race, you felt physically ill, and the rest of the week, you wanted to stay in bed and watch your favorite series on Netflix. You feel ashamed because after so many years, a different accident shouldn't have impacted you this way.

As your counselor, I'd remind you this was a normal response. Triggers can come from any situation or scenario that's like a trauma we've previously experienced. Even a smell, a sensation, or a time of year when we experienced trauma can become a trigger. I would tell you that your brain was trying to keep you safe, and you went into fight mode, then freeze mode, to try to resume a sense of safety.

Become A Noticer

I designed an online trauma course, After Trauma Hope, to help teach some of these concepts. One of my favorite parts of creating that course was interviewing therapists about trauma. Mazi Robinson has been a licensed professional counselor for over 18 years, and she talked with me about how important it is to let go of shame.

She reminds us, "You are NOT damaged or bad, your body is simply trying to bring you back to a sense of safety."[12]

She said the most significant skill we can teach ourselves is self-awareness. Be a noticer. Mazi said she often reminds her clients that as you begin to notice your response to triggers, it's important to get curious and observe, but not judge. Use it as research. She compared it to when we Google something. We're googling something out of curiosity to find an answer, not to judge an answer.

What did you see, taste, smell, hear, or experience that caused your reaction?

What emotions are you feeling?

What are you feeling in your body?

Is this a real present threat, or based on your past circumstances?

What would make you feel safe again?

Did I mention I like happy feelings? I'm not one who wants to take a deep dive into my feelings. (*Fascinating, I know, because of the line of work I'm in. What can I say? I am fascinating!*) I could hold space for your feelings all day, but I don't want to notice my own. And when I do experience a trauma trigger, I just want to pretend it didn't happen.

But I started to let myself become a noticer. To look at my responses without shame. To look at my physical and emotional reactions to situations and ask some questions about what I'm feeling or experiencing.

Remember how I told you that I came to realize I could check many of the big "T" trauma boxes like war, tornado, and accident? During that time, I began to let myself become more self-aware. And in doing so, I recognized I had a large "trauma" bucket capacity, but I needed to drain some of the bucket.

I began to pay attention when I had a big emotional reaction to something small. I'd ask myself what was happening that triggered this reaction. How could it tie to a situation of past trauma in my life?

I noticed my heart rate would go higher when I heard a chain-saw, because it reminded me of the weeks after the tornado, when I was doing trauma care. All you heard were chainsaws going as people tried to unbury their houses.

I noticed how my heart rate would shoot up, and I would go into flight mode and want to run out of the building if a piece of heavy construction equipment happened to drive by and cause the ground to shake a little. My body would think I needed to get out because I was experiencing another earthquake. It took work, even with my counseling training, to notice this about myself. I could help others work through it, but it was hard to pause and notice because I just wanted to move past things, get over it, not be impacted.

But noticing brought freedom. I could tell when my normally easy-going self experienced a trigger that made me irritable or on edge. I now could work on ways to remind my brain and body that I did not need to stay in survival mode, that it was safe.

You may have wrestled. You may be limping. But you're still here.

I want you to free yourself from the question, "Why can't I just get it together?" Friend, you may have been hurt in an instant, or over a life-time of instances, but your body can find healing. In the following chapters, we'll dive deeper into our fight, flight, freeze, or fawn responses to trauma. You'll begin to learn what your typi-cal reaction is to a stress or trauma trigger and how these can both serve you and leave you stuck. I'll share more practical tips and tricks on what to do when you have been triggered into that fight/flight/freeze/fawn mode. What do you do when your brain ineffectively tries to bring you back to a sense of safety?

Walk with a Limp

Experiencing a trauma trigger can feel very frustrating and harmful because it brings back a past event and can make it feel like you're experiencing it again in the present. My freshman year of college, I had an unfortunate injury from a Nerf hockey game.

I know, right? Who gets hurt playing Nerf hockey? What's even more embarrassing is that it was a workers' compensation situation because I was injured serving as a camp counselor for adults with differing abilities. I had to fill out ALL the paperwork because surgery was required for my injury. Do you know how embarrassing it feels to write source of injury: NERF HOCKEY!

It took a while for surgery to be approved, so I walked for a bit with a pretty significant limp due to the pain. After surgery, I went to physical therapy. I loved the part of physical therapy where you lie there, and they wrap you in giant ice packs, but I hated all the rest. I remember the therapist having me walk around the room. They kept instructing me to walk without a limp. But I had limped for so long that my brain didn't know how to not do it. I kept walking around in circles, limping. It took a long time, slowly continuing to take baby steps, to walk without that limp. And still, twenty years later, when I'm tired or have worked out too hard, the limp comes back.

Your trauma limp may be there forever, and you may find it sensitive to triggers. But you can learn to walk smoothly one baby step at a time, with that limp showing itself less over time.

I think of Jacob from the Bible when I think about walking with a limp. Genesis 32:24–31 tells us:

> And Jacob was left alone. And a man wrestled with
> him until the breaking of the day. When the man saw
> that he did not prevail against Jacob, he touched his
> hip socket, and Jacob's hip was put out of joint as he

wrestled with him. Then he said, "Let me go, for the day has broken." But Jacob said, "I will not let you go unless you bless me." And he said to him, "What is your name?" And he said, "Jacob." Then he said, "Your name shall no longer be called Jacob, but Israel, for you have striven with God and with men, and have prevailed." Then Jacob asked him, "Please tell me your name." But he said, "Why is it that you ask my name?" And there he blessed him. So Jacob called the name of the place Peniel, saying, "For I have seen God face to face, and yet my life has been delivered." The sun rose upon him as he passed Penuel, limping because of his hip.

Genesis 32:24–31

Jacob went through a wrestling match with God, and that caused a limp. In your journey to healing, you may find yourself wrestling with God. Wrestling with doubt. Wrestling with fear. Wrestling with questions. Wrestling is okay. In fact, It's good! It's my prayer that you find comfort in this story. After the wrestling, Jacob may have walked with a limp, but He also received a blessing and a change of name.

Trauma will change you. The limp may come and go. But I pray the time comes when you can say you have seen God, and your life has been delivered.

Heart Work: Permission to Limp (and Still Belong)

Welcome to the chapter where we *fall on our backs in the snow, twice,* and decide to start noticing what made us slip. You're here, which means you're brave—even if it doesn't feel like it. And if you've ever asked yourself, "What is wrong with me?" . . . this section is especially for you.

Let's start releasing shame and practicing self-awareness— one gentle question at a time.

1. What's Your Black Ice?

PROMPT: Recall a moment that knocked the wind out of you, and you didn't see it coming? Maybe it was something small that caused a very big internal reaction.

"Everything looked fine . . . until it wasn't. I didn't expect to feel _____ when _____ happened."

Even if you don't fully understand why it hit so hard, write it anyway. You might uncover some black ice that's been hiding in plain sight.

2. Become a Noticer

We're not judging. We're just Googling your internal landscape.

JOURNALING PROMPTS: The next time you experience a big emotional or physical reaction, ask yourself:

- What just happened?
- What did I see, smell, hear, taste, or feel?
- What emotions came up and possibly out?
- Where did I feel it in my body?
- Is this a real, current threat—or is my brain remembering something old?

Now practice here with a recent moment:

"I noticed I reacted when _____. I felt it in my _____. I think my body was trying to _____."

_____

_____

_____

_____

_____

_____

_____

_____

_____

3. Triggers Are Not Weaknesses

REFLECTION: Write a list of three things that have triggered you—emotionally, spiritually, physically, relationally. They can be tiny or enormous.

Then write beside each:

"This was my brain trying to keep me safe. Not me failing."

Example:

- 🌿 Loud yelling → *My brain thought it was danger.*
- 🌿 News story about war → *My body remembered Ukraine.*
- 🌿 Crowded room → *This felt like I might lose control again.*

- 🌿 .... → ....
- 🌿 .... → ....
- 🌿 .... → ....

4. From Shame to Curiosity

Let's rewrite some common "should" statements:

- 🌿 "I should be over this by now." → *Healing isn't a race. I'm still walking it out.*
- 🌿 "Why can't I get it together?" → *Because I've been through hard things, and I'm learning.*
- 🌿 "I should not feel this way." → *My body's response makes perfect sense.*

Now write your own:

"I used to think ...., but now I'm learning ...."

5. Broken Chairs & Cozy Counseling

Pretend you're sitting across from the world's most compassionate, curious counselor *(you can picture me with a coffee in hand in my cozy office)*.

PROMPT: What would you tell them about how you've been feeling lately? What reaction do you wish someone would validate?

Then complete this sentence:

"If someone could hear me right now, I'd want them to say _____."

_____

_____

_____

_____

6. Walk with a Limp

You may have wrestled. You may be limping. But you're still here.

PROMPT: Write about your limp. What shows up in your life when you're tired, triggered, or worn out? What makes it better? What's the blessing that has come even through the struggle?

Try: "My limp looks like _____. But my story also includes _____."

_____

_____

_____

7. From Wrestling to Blessing

Jacob limped after he wrestled. But he also walked forward, changed, re-named, and not alone.

REFLECTION QUESTION: What have you wrestled with most in your healing journey: God? People? Fear? Shame? Doubt?

Write a prayer of hope to go alongside your limp.

It can be short, honest, messy, or sacred. Something like:

"God, I don't understand _____, but I still want to see You in it."

"Help me walk forward, even when I limp."

You don't have to "get it together" to keep healing.

Just keep walking—limp and all.

Take a breath. Warm up from the fall. And know you aren't walking alone.

CHAPTER 5

FIGHT, FLIGHT, FREEZE, OR FAWN

There's a mean dog in our neighborhood. I know exactly the point in our daily walk where I must walk by its house. The dog is enormous, has a huge, intimidating bark, and it seems, to me at least, it has many sharp teeth that could take a big bite out of my leg.

The dog is typically on a chain, but I often worry the chain isn't enough to hold it back from eating us for breakfast. I will never forget the day it wasn't on a chain. As the sun rose, my sister, our friend, Beth, and I were out for an early morning walk. I had yet to have my morning coffee! The dog did what it always did, barked, and showed its teeth. But this day was different. Its chain had snapped, and it was coming for us.

The three of us each had a different response. My sister screamed. She yelled like she was going to fight that dog with her words, and she was ready to fight. My friend Beth, who'd had a bad experience with a dog bite, began running. And I just froze. I tend to freeze, stay calm in an emergency, and react later.

I had this same reaction a different time in Italy. This time it wasn't a dog, but a crow. Yes, you read that right. It was a giant, buzzard-sized crow. My friends Ariana, Lucia, and I sat eating at a restaurant by a river. When we pulled up to the restaurant, we noticed a large crow pecking at the window. The workers and other people didn't seem to think this was strange. When we sat down at our cute little outside table to order, it no longer felt so pretty and cute when that crow with its large, strong beak flew right beside me and looked at me with its beady eyes. What kind of restaurant has a pet crow?

However, I will say that was the best pizza of my entire life! I still dream about it and have never had a slice I loved more than the one I ate beside the crow that day. But as we got ready to leave, the crow followed us. We watched it fly over and start pecking the top of my friend Lucia's car—like it would peck its way through the car. Lucia dropped the car keys to shoo it away, while my friend Ariana put down the pizza leftovers to try to help.

Next thing we knew, the crow was trying to fly off with the car keys. Lucia went into fight mode. She was going to get the keys from the crow. As she entered fight mode, the crow started flying at her, attacking her back. She continued screaming, waving her arms, and fighting off the crow.

Ariana, meanwhile, returned to grab the pizza box because that was still the best pizza of our lives, and her priority was to protect those leftovers. Then she began to run away. And I just stood there, frozen. Like the time with the loose dog, I just watched it all go down, not moving or doing anything. These two examples—the dog and the crow—show how everyone can respond differently to the same trauma.

There are four natural responses to trauma: fight, flight, freeze, or fawn. When you're triggered about an old trauma, or experience a new trauma, your brain and body may engage in one of these natural responses. Fight, flight, freeze, or fawn are also survival mechanisms that try to protect us from more trauma. But we can get stuck in any one these responses.

As I deeply studied these responses over the past few years, I began to see the impact staying stuck in these modes was having on people around the world. I began to teach people about fight, flight, freeze, and fawn, and how these responses impact our brains and bodies, and I could see the lightbulb go on for them. They began to feel empowered as they recognized their typical reaction to triggers. When I teach about fight, flight, freeze, and fawn, I ask people to guess what each other's typical reaction to trauma or stress is. There's usually some laughing as they point out what they think, especially for those who typically react with a fight reaction.

Let's dive into each of these trauma responses.

Fighter

You are a fighter. Imagine this: you're at a coffee shop, waiting in a long line. You've had a rough day at work and need that two o'clock coffee treat, so you decide to wait out the line. The barista seems new, and the people in front of you have all the complicated orders.

You wait, and wait, and wait.

When it's finally your turn, you order your coffee exactly how you want it. Caramel latte, extra hot, steamed breve with cinnamon powder on top. When you go to get your coffee at the bar, you realize your coffee was mistakenly taken by someone else, but now you don't have time for the barista to make another.

You instantly feel your blood pressure rising. Your heart rate is increasing. You're more than agitated. You are angry! Your jaw tightens, you feel that pit in your stomach, and you must ball your fists because you want to use them.

You are a fighter.

When the fight response is triggered

PHYSICAL RESPONSE	EMOTIONAL RESPONSE
Increased heart rate	Anger
Heightened blood pressure	Agitated
Release of cortisol and adrenaline	Crying
Tightened jaw	Urge to punch something or someone
Upset stomach	Urge to yell

This may seem like a benign reason for your fight response to be triggered. However, this is a big deal if you're a coffee lover like me! Especially if it's your first coffee of the day! Your own fight response might have been triggered as a child if you were continually degraded and yelled at by a parent. It might be triggered now because you feel unsafe in a relationship that reminds you of how you felt as that little child. It might be triggered even by watching a news story that reminds you of a painful time in your past when you felt unsafe emotionally, physically, relationally, or spiritually.

When your fight reaction is triggered, you may notice your heart racing and your blood pressure rising. It's almost like you can see and feel the release of the stress chemicals, cortisol and adrenaline, racing through your body. You may feel like you want to throw up. You may be so angry you want to yell—or punch someone or something. You may burst into tears, feel extreme rage, or become physically agitated.

This is your body's fight song.

Flight

If this is your typical trauma response, you might call yourself a flight risk. When your stress reaction and past trauma are triggered—you are out of here! You may be physically present in a room or situation, but you already know the escape route. If this is you, imagine that you're in a big conference room in a meeting, and you feel criticized by your boss in front of the rest of the group.

You don't fight back; you simply pick up your things and walk out quietly. In a conflict, you walk away. When the going gets hard, you find yourself going. You want to take flight because you want to escape or avoid both emotional and physical pain. You also may find yourself escaping to compulsions, like organizing, cleaning, obsessive running, etc.

When the flight response is triggered

PHYSICAL RESPONSE	EMOTIONAL RESPONSE
Increased heart rate	Fear
Rush of cortisol and adrenaline	Heightened anxiety
Rapid breathing	Sense of urgency to escape
Dilated pupils	Feeling of powerlessness
Muscle tension	Emotional disconnection
Sweating	Feelings of guilt/shame
Tunnel vision	Feeling of dread

This stress response tends to be one of mine. I may not physically leave a room or situation, but I can run to comfort to calm my heart emotionally with the best of them. An emotional "runner," when triggered, may find their heart rate increasing, a rush of cortisol and adrenaline in their body, and their breathing rapid just like one who is physically running. However, the response is different from the fighter in a key way. Fighters tend to go towards whatever the trigger is in anger, while runners focus on escape. We may start to sweat, experience tunnel vision, find our muscles tensing, and we want to get out of there. If we cannot physically flee, we will emotionally flee. *(Netflix marathon anyone? Or scrolling social media until our finger gets sore and our brain is turned off entirely?)* The runner has a sense of urgency and will try to escape at any cost.

Frozen

You are a freezer. You don't find yourself running or fighting—you just stop. You appear to be right there, but you've checked out. In the movie *Frozen*, Elsa is an excellent example of this. *(Tell me you want to belt out the song "Let it Go" at the top of your lungs!)* She was afraid her powers would hurt someone else, so in her fear, she locked herself away in the palace and didn't go anywhere.

The other trauma responses tend to come with quick action and response. When you freeze, you have a moment to assess the situation. But that benefit is quickly lost if you're never able to unfreeze.

When the Freeze Response is Triggered

PHYSICAL RESPONSE	EMOTIONAL RESPONSE
Decreased Heart Rate	Fear
Numbness in your body	Numbness in your emotions
Immobile—unable to move	Feeling of helplessness
Holding your breath	Frustration due to inability to act
Having trouble speaking	Anxiety
Dissociation	Shame and Guilt

Fight and flight responses tend to come with an increased heart rate, while those experiencing the freeze response tend to experience a decreased rate. Freezing is often described as a feeling of going numb, physically and emotionally. The freeze response can make your body feel like you cannot move at all, or like you have cement blocks holding your feet in place. Freezers describe a feeling of paralysis regarding their situation. Instead of moving towards action, they may disassociate from what's happening as they struggle to find movement.

If you have experienced this, you may even feel like you've lost your speaking ability. Not only can your body feel frozen in place but so are your words. Emotionally, you may feel afraid, numb, and helpless. You may want to act, but can't, causing feelings of frustration, anxiety, shame, and guilt. "Why did I not do something? Why did I react with inaction instead of action?"

If you struggle with shame and guilt over your inaction, remind yourself that you were acting in your body's natural stress response. Don't let shame and guilt keep you frozen even more. Understand that your inaction is simply a trauma response and continue to seek healing rather than ruminate on what you should or shouldn't have done in the situation.

Fawn

Fawning is a stress and trauma–triggered response that many people may not know about. If you experience the fawn response after stress or trauma, you may have been voted most likely to please people in your high school yearbook. When you go into the fawn response, you do everything you can to make every-one happy.

You intensely focus on meeting other people's needs, often to the detriment of your own needs. Picture this: you're a parent of toddlers and a newborn, and you find yourself with no sleep, changing diapers, and cleaning up some unidentifiable sticky substance on the counters. Your stress level is high, and you find yourself triggered. How do you cope? You go out of your way to ensure everyone in your family is pleased and happy, even if you haven't taken the time to shower in days. You prioritize maintaining harmony and avoiding conflict at all costs.

It can be hard to admit and recognize this is a coping mechanism because it's easily disguised as service to others.

When the Fawn Stress Response is Triggered

PHYSICAL RESPONSE	EMOTIONAL RESPONSE
Higher heart rate	Codependency on others
Cortisol levels rising	Struggle with boundaries
Adrenaline rising (stress hormones)	Feelings of shame
Shallow breathing	Suppression of feelings and desire
A pit in the stomach/digestive issues	Lack of Emotional Regulation
Hypervigilance	Feelings
Muscle tension	Lack of authenticity

The fawn stress response can come with higher heart rates and cortisol levels. People may have no idea you're experiencing a trauma trigger because you're good at suppressing your feelings and work hard to make sure everyone else is okay. Even though others may not know what's happening, your body does. You may experience shallow breathing and a pit in your stomach. As someone who tends to fawn, I can feel that pit in my stomach just writing about it. Your body is hypervigilant, almost like you're waiting on edge because you're trying not to disappoint someone. Your muscles will tense, and you may feel like you've overworked in a workout class. (If you're a fawn, I bet you're the best person in the workout class because you don't want to disappoint the trainer even though your body may be distressed!)

Those who have the fawn response can become co-dependent on others. Your emotions are my emotions. The way you feel directly impacts how I feel. Maintaining boundaries can be very hard *(raising my hand with you here on this one!)* Fawns can suppress their feelings and desires with the best of them. You may not know how to be authentic around people because you can lose sight of yourself. You're constantly asking is everyone okay and if not, what can you do to change that?

Where do you see yourself?

You probably experience some of each of these reactions as you go through life. Even if your typical stress response is to be a fawn, trying to please everyone, you may have that moment when the fighter comes out of you. While we usually do have one or two typical responses, it's important to know about all these ways to respond to trauma so we can observe our reactions. The next chapter will discuss how these reactions can serve us without us staying stuck in them.

There are hiking trails right by my house I love to go to. They're relatively easy to navigate and well-marked for me, the girl who could get lost easily anywhere. Those trails are a happy, safe place for me. One day I was hiking and found myself stepping on a giant poisonous snake. I didn't know I could physically jump that high, but with this snake sighting, and hearing it slither under my shoe, I was airborne like I had a jet pack. My body went into flight mode. I jumped high and ran far. I wanted to get away from that snake as far and as fast as I could.

From then on, I was diligent in watching the trail, looking for any signs of a slithering snake. Just because there was one that time on the trail didn't mean they would be there every time I hiked but I became much more observant. As you learn about the different responses to trauma, you can become more observant. Rather than responding with shame towards yourself for your reactions, you can begin asking yourself questions. When you find yourself having a big reaction to small situation, you can recognize you're stuck in a stress response. Then you can take action to keep the stress hormones from staying stuck in your body and heart. Do you recognize which of these reactions tends to be your response to stress and trauma?

I developed a quiz *(it's not scientifically statistical and all of that, so don't expect statistical analysis and charts and such—I hated statistics class far too much for that.)* online at stressresponsequiz.com because I wanted people to have a fun way to figure out which was their typical stress response. As I developed the quiz, I correlated the answers to which Bible character, Disney character, and '80s TV sitcom character was similar to each stress response.

In case you're curious, I'll include those not-so-statistically-proven results in this chapter for fun. (Remember, I like to make things fun!) Turn the page!

Stress Response Quiz Results

YOU ARE A FIGHTER!

If you were a Disney character, you would be: Simba from *The Lion King*

Initially, he was a scared lion cub who was triggered by the trauma of the death of His father, which He blamed himself for. But when push came to shove, he confronted Scar and fought for the Pride Lands. He was a fighter.

If you were a Bible character, you would be: Moses

Moses got himself into trouble when he saw an Egyptian beating up one of his own Hebrew people. He got so angry, wanted justice, and not only fought the Egyptian, but he also killed him. Don't worry, I'm not saying you'll reach this level—but I bet you do feel a need inside of you to fight for justice when you've seen wrong.

If you were an '80s TV sitcom character you would be: Dorothy from *The Golden Girls*

She was a feisty one! With her sharp wit and quick tongue, she didn't shy away from conflict or speaking her mind!

YOU TAKE FLIGHT!

If you were a Disney character you would be: Belle from *Beauty and the Beast*

After encountering the Beast and being afraid (*I mean I would be!*) she escaped the castle. This was her initial fight response. Later she does return, but I don't want to spoil the story for you if you haven't seen it.

If you were a Bible character you would be: Jonah

You can read a whole book in the Bible about Him fleeing. He'd been asked by God to go to Ninevah to share with them about God, but He didn't want to go, so he ran the other way and somehow ended up in the belly of a whale.

If you were an '80s TV sitcom character you would: Frasier Crane from *Cheers*

He flees to Boston after his marriage ends. He can also avoid conflict by using humor to defect. That's one of the skills used in fleeing.

YOU ARE A FREEZER!

If you were a Disney character, you would be: Elsa, of course, from *Frozen*

There's a whole movie about her being frozen. She isolates herself and doesn't leave her room because she fears her powers and doesn't want to be a danger to anyone.

If you were a Bible character, you would be: Daniel

In Daniel 10:7–9, we read that Daniel had a vision from God, and in his fear, it says he lost his strength and couldn't move. He fell on his face like he was in a deep sleep. He froze, and his body responded.

If you were an '80s TV sitcom character, you would be: Alex Keaton from *Family Ties*

He usually showed himself to be confident and assertive, but when conflict or stress came, there were moments he would demonstrate a freeze–like response before he'd regain his composure.

YOU ARE A FAWN.

If you were a Disney character, you would be: Cinderella from *Cinderella*

During her trauma, she worked hard to please everyone. She was gentle, kind, and accommodating even when dealing with her evil stepsisters.

If you were a Bible character, you would be: Esther

She wanted to please the king. She asked the royal advisors what he liked, listening to their counsel. She even hid her Jewish identity to please him.

If you were an '80s TV sitcom character, you would be: DJ Tanner of *Full House*

As the oldest, she always tried to be responsible and helpful. As the responsible older sister, she did everything to keep harmony in the house.

Heart Work: Stress Responses and Other Superpowers in Disguise

Trauma has its language—sometimes it barks at you like a big dog or flies at your head like an angry crow. Sometimes, you fight. Sometimes, you run. Sometimes, you freeze. Sometimes, you try to people-please your way to safety. However you've responded—then or now—you're not broken. You're wired for survival.

This chapter helped you name those responses. Now, let's take a moment to explore what your nervous system has been trying to say, without shame or side-eyes.

1. Black Ice, Big Dog, or Buzzard Crow?

PROMPT: What moment have you recently felt unexpectedly triggered—emotionally, physically, or spiritually? Maybe something seemed small (a smell, a tone of voice, a moment of chaos), but it made your insides do something big.

Try this:

"I thought I was just _____, but then I felt _____, and I didn't know why."

"Looking back, I think I may have been triggered because _____."

Remember—just naming it *is* the brave step.

2. What's Your Default Survival Style?

Now that you've read through the four Fs, which one do you *most often* use when you're triggered or under stress?

Circle one:

- ❦ Fight
- ❦ Flight
- ❦ Freeze
- ❦ Fawn

Now answer:

- ❦ What do you like about that response? (It protected me, helped me cope, gave me space . . .)

_____

_____

_____

_____

- ❦ What makes it hard to live from that response long–term?

_____

_____

_____

_____

3. Stress Response Inventory

Let's make a personal mini "symptom tracker" to notice your cues (no statistics needed—we're not traumatizing you with flashbacks of stats class).

When I'm triggered, I tend to experience:

PHYSICAL SIGNS	EMOTIONAL SIGNS	COMMON TRIGGERS
(ex, rapid heartbeat)	*(ex, shame, panic)*	*(ex, loud voices, crowds, loneliness)*

Look at your list. What do you notice?

4. From Shame to Curiosity

Complete these prompts gently, without judgment:

- ✿ "I used to think I was weak because I _____ , but now I know my brain was protecting me."

- ✿ "A pattern I want to observe more compassionately is _____ ."

- ✿ "Next time I'm triggered, I want to remember _____ ."

For example:

- ✿ I used to think I was weak because I would shake after a loud noise, but now I know my brain was protecting me.

- ✿ A pattern I want to observe more compassionately is when I get flooded with a feeling of wanting to hide in a room of people.

- ✿ Next time I'm triggered, I want to remember this is a normal response to trauma.

5. Walking with a Limp

Like stepping on a snake (hard pass) or walking after surgery, trauma recovery may come with a limp. It doesn't mean you're broken. It means you're healing.

Reflection Prompt: "My limp looks like _____ , but it reminds me that I've survived _____ ."

Then try: "One blessing I've gained in this healing journey is _____ ."

For example:

My limp looks like a fear of relationships, but it reminds me that I've survived an abusive situation.

One blessing I've gained in this healing journey is an ability to understand others.

6. Becoming a Noticer

Next time you feel "off," pause and try this simple 5-step practice *(bonus points for using a soft voice with yourself)*:

1. What's happening around me right now?
2. What am I feeling in my body?
3. What am I feeling in my emotions?
4. Does this feel familiar?
5. Is there something I can do to feel 5% safer right now?

You don't have to fix it all. You just have to notice.

You are becoming a noticer. And that, my friend, is where freedom begins.

CHAPTER 6

IS THIS STILL SERVING YOU?

I don't know about you, but when I go to a restaurant, the service really matters to me. Have you ever had an experience where you had the best food in the world, but the service was horrible? Maybe they got your order wrong twice, were rude, or never filled your drink even once? If the food is bad but the server does a great job—is attentive, kind and comes to check on you just enough times *(and might I add doesn't ask you if you want a box because you fully plan on eating that whole giant burger even if they think you should not!)*, then I'm much more likely to return to that restaurant to give the food another try.

In the previous chapter, we talked about fight/flight/freeze/ fawn responses and the ways they manifest in our brains and bodies when we experience a stress or trauma trigger. These responses can be very important and beneficial in moments of high intensity and stress. Think of them as the good servers at the restaurant. Life may be handing you meatloaf that's too cold and french-fries that aren't salty enough, but your stress response mechanisms are serving you well in the moment. They make sure you have exactly what you need, plenty of drink refills included *(sorry for the extended cheesy metaphor, but I love a good cheesy metaphor! So, thanks for playing along.)*

But there does come a time when these responses are no longer serving you. It goes from good for you to bad for your brain and body to stay in that heightened state. So, it's helpful to learn to notice when these response mechanisms are serving you and when they're causing you to become stuck.

Let me give you a real-life example to help flesh this out. This week I got a call from a friend. Her daughter had woken up with a stomach bug. Truthfully—the stomach bug is enough to awaken a fear response in all of us. *(I don't know about you, but I've heard the old wives' tale that drinking grape juice keeps you from getting the bug. So, you better believe sometimes, even if I just hear about the stomach bug going around, I'll be chugging Welch's grape juice like there's no tomorrow. It's probably some myth spread by the grape juice companies for marketing—but I'm here for it!)*

My friend asked me to pray because she said she felt simply paralyzed. Frozen. Her trauma response was to immediately feel like she couldn't function. The problem was, she couldn't stay frozen. Not only did she need to attend to the needs of her daughter, but the family was leaving for a trip, and she needed to do all the things moms need to do to get ready for a trip.

As we talked, it became clear the freeze response wasn't just because there was throw up involved. Her daughter being sick was a trigger for her. This family had dealt with a premature birth that involved a very intense NICU stay. It broke my heart when my friend shared she'd once found her daughter not breathing at home. Talk about a helpless feeling as a parent!

Now, any illness of a child triggered the reminders of those past traumas. The similar feelings. The fears about how to protect her heart and her child. The frozen response was perfectly normal from this trauma trigger of a child being ill.

I was able to point out that what was happening in her body was a response to past trauma. I first reminded my friend not to feel shame for feeling paralyzed and stuck—that was her brain's amazing way of trying to find safety. At the risk of sounding like a broken record, I want to remind you of that as well. Shame is so sneaky and is one of the things that can make us stay stuck. When we feel dumb or like we shouldn't respond in certain ways, this doesn't serve us. But how could I help her not stay stuck there?

In graduate school, I learned some practical things to do when you recognize you're becoming stuck in fight/flight/freeze/fawn mode. To be honest—I thought it was a bit hokey then. They were simple tools; how could they really work? But eventually I started having to practice them myself and I found that they really worked.

Breathing? That's naturally something we all do, so how could this help?

Using the five senses? I mean, how could touching, tasting, and smelling something really help anyone?

Moving my body? That felt like a far reach as something that could help me when I was having a horrific flashback of the accident and trying to drive, or something made the earth shake a little and made me want to run out of a building. We'll talk more about these tools and how to use them in pages to come because I want you to have them in your trauma response toolbelt.

Are you stuck?

I've been stuck in a few different places and situations over the course of my life. My least favorite experience as a camp counselor was caving. There was something about donning that helmet with the headlamp, knowing I was about to take kids into a tight dark underground hole that I was responsible for getting them into—and out of—that made me uneasy. There were times in the caving expedition that I wasn't sure I knew where I was going. There were times when we were in such a tight place, I was sure I had us stuck forever. My flight stress response is triggered just thinking about it; I just had to wipe my sweaty palms.

Sometimes we don't realize we're in a stuck place. Maybe you aren't sure if you're in the place where your fight/flight/freeze/fawn response is serving you right now, or you're stuck and need some release. Recognizing you're stuck can help you begin to take action to release and regain a sense of control.

FIGHT RESPONSE

Wondering if you're stuck in the fight response? Here are some starter questions you can ask yourself that will help you begin to recognize if maybe you're responding to a situation because you're stuck in the heightened state of your triggered fight response.

- 🌿 Am I feeling anger that's unusual or escalated for the situation I'm in?

- 🌿 Do I feel the intense need to prove myself?

- 🌿 Am I feeling a sense of aggression I cannot seem to shake?

- 🌿 What is my body stance right now? Is my body tight, my jaw clenched, do I feel tension in my shoulders?

- 🌿 Do I feel the need to fight, either physically or verbally?

FLIGHT RESPONSE

Wondering if you're stuck in the flight response? Here are some starter questions you can ask yourself that will help you begin to recognize if maybe you're responding to a situation because you're stuck in the heightened state of your triggered flight response.

- Do I feel like running away from this person, conversation, situation?
- Am I looking for my escape route?
- Am I distracting myself with something else—like work, sex, relationships, food, or scrolling?
- Do I feel like I cannot relax my brain or my body?
- Are my thoughts constantly racing and I cannot seem to calm or quiet them?

FREEZE RESPONSE

Wondering if you're stuck in the freeze response? Here are some starter questions you can ask yourself that will help you begin to recognize if maybe you're responding to a situation because you're stuck in the heightened state of your triggered freeze response.

- Do I feel disconnected or zoned out from a situation? Do I feel disconnected from the people in my life?
- Am I feeling nothing at all because I'm numb emotionally?
- Does my body feel heavy, like I'm trying to walk through cement?
- Am I struggling to make decisions?
- Is it hard for me to articulate my thoughts?
- Do I feel detached from life in such a way that I feel like I'm watching a movie of someone else's life?

FAWN RESPONSE

Wondering if you're stuck in the fawn response? Here are some starter questions you can ask yourself that will help you begin to recognize if maybe you're responding to a situation because you're stuck in the heightened state of your triggered fawn response.

- Am I agreeing to do this to please others or do I really want to do it?
- Am I making everyone else's needs a priority above my own?
- Am I afraid to set boundaries because I'm worried about how the person will respond?
- Am I losing my own sense of self?
- Do I find myself apologizing for everything?

I don't know about you, but reading these questions brought about a good moment of self-evaluation for me. It helped me recognize some areas where I may be stuck in fight/flight/freeze/fawn mode and need to take steps to help reduce my stress response hormones. Sometimes it can be challenging to put a mirror up to our hearts because we don't want to acknowledge the things we (might) see. It's important that we get brave here, look in the mirror and see where we may need to take some of the action steps that we'll talk about in the next chapter.

Heart Work: Stuck Isn't Forever: A Self-Check for the Fight, Flight, Freeze, or Fawned-Out

Sometimes your stress response shows up like an over-attentive waiter, refilling your drink every five seconds even though you're good—and now your sweet tea has spilled all over the table. The problem isn't that your body responded with fight, flight, freeze, or fawn. The problem is the helpful server refuses to take the hint you're full and don't need another refill.

Let's gently take inventory. No shame. No judgment. Just noticing.

1. What's Been "Serving" You . . . and What's Not Anymore?

Take a moment to think about which of the four trauma responses you tend to lean into most (fight, flight, freeze, or fawn).

- Lately, which response has shown up most often in your story.
- How has that response served you well?
- Where might it be keeping you stuck?

2. Dear Body, Thanks for Showing Up

Our bodies really are trying their best. Even when we freeze. Even when we bolt. Even when we people-please our way into exhaustion. Write a short thank-you note to your body for how it's protected you.

Start with:

Dear Body,

Thanks for . . .

---

3. Pause and Check the Mirror

Let's use a few of those reflection questions as a journaling moment.

- Is there an area of my life where I feel stuck right now? What might be underneath that?
- Where am I acting out of fear, not freedom?
- What would it look like to gently walk myself toward safety and a sense of calm in this area?

4. Reminder: Stuck is Not Forever

What is one tiny baby step you could take this week to help your brain and body move out of "stuck"? *(It could be as small as taking a deep breath, going for a walk, saying "no" to one thing, or speaking kindly to yourself in the mirror—without confusing yourself for your twin.)*

You don't have to get un-stuck all at once. You just have to notice when you're stuck and choose one small step that will take you forward. Let's give that trauma server a good tip for keeping you alive—and then gently ask them to clock out for the night.

CHAPTER 7

WHAT YOUR BRAIN AND BODY CAN DO

Marathon and Math Problems

Marathon and math problems. Two things that make my body and brain hurt just thinking about them. I wouldn't go so far as to say it was trauma, but I can still picture sitting at our oval-shaped oak kitchen table doing high school math problems, crying because I just couldn't seem to understand what my engineer dad was trying to say as he helped me. And I can still feel the pain in my legs and lungs when I think about my body trying to finish the marathon I didn't adequately train for.

Even though both situations were challenging, my brain and body worked for me. I was able to figure out the math problems, *eventually. (And might I add I have never once been asked in my real life to calculate the sine and cosine of a triangle, but I'm breaking out in hives right now just thinking about it!)* And, yes, I did finish that marathon *eventually.* Our brains and bodies can do amazing, hard things. Our brains and bodies also store our hard experiences, and we can experience the aftereffects of that.

There are ways you can use your brain and body together to help find a way to experience a regained sense of control after your brain and body have experienced a trauma or stress trigger. Since trauma occurs when you feel unsafe physically, emotionally, relationally, or spiritually, it can be helpful for you to feel like you can grasp some control in regaining your sense of safety.

It can be easy to wonder why our body is being triggered, or why we're still experiencing that stomachache that never seems to go away, or the knot in our shoulders. Just remember, your brain and body are doing their jobs, they just happen to be clocking in some overtime.

I was cooking today, and my smoke alarm went off. Because my apartment is small, it seems whenever I turn the oven on at a high temperature, the smoke alarm goes off but that doesn't always mean there's a fire as the root cause. *(Ironically, last week, when I caught something on fire for REAL and had to throw flour on the stove eye to smother out the flames, the smoke alarm didn't make a peep!)* Our brains work the same way. Our brains sense a trigger, and alarm bells start going off in our bodies. It doesn't have to be the actual traumatic scenario to cause the brain to start firing and the body to start reacting.

Let me give you an example of someone I worked with. They'd experienced a very traumatic birth experience with their third child. Both her and the child had almost died in the experience, and it was a very hard physical recovery. The hospital where this occurred used a certain type of cleaner. Years later, when Ashley *(I changed the names of those involved in these chapters)* would smell anything that resembled the cleaner they used in the hospital, her heart would begin to race, and she'd get a migraine and need to lay down. The smell triggered her brain back to the traumatic birth experience, her body remembered, which resulted in her having to lay in a dark room to get rid of her migraine. We worked on using some of the techniques we'll talk about to help her when she experienced this trigger, helping her brain and body to ground in the present moment.

The Body's Traffic Cop

Every day, I go with my twin sister and sit in the school pickup lines with her. *(Yes, I said lines, she has four kids in four different schools!)* If you have trauma in your mind when you think about a school pick-up line, I understand. I sit with my sister to make it FUN, but wow, it's always a whole thing. We laugh because it doesn't matter what time we get there—we somehow always get the kids at the same time.

And then there are the school traffic cops. I have difficulty understanding their signals for some reason, and I always seem to do the wrong thing. Get in the lane they aren't pointing me towards. Going when I'm supposed to be stopping. Then there was the time I was happily reading my e-book and missed that the traffic in front of me had been long gone, and all the people behind me were getting furious at me. It's essential for me to pay attention to the traffic cop telling me when to go, where to go, and when to stop or slow.

Our bodies and brains have their own traffic directors, and to be honest, it can sometimes be hard to figure out what they're signaling us to do. Other times, our bodies just respond as if on autopilot. Two different traffic cops are directing our bodies: the parasympathetic nervous system and the sympathetic nervous system. To put this simply *(because, as you may have noticed, I love a good analogy)*, the parasympathetic nervous system is the traffic cop putting his hand up to stop or slow things down. It's the part of your body trying to return to normal functioning. In contrast, the sympathetic nervous system tells you to put all systems on go, like the people behind me honking, because we need to move the line.

The fancy people at the Cleveland Health Clinic describe it this way: "Your sympathetic and parasympathetic nervous systems have opposite but complementary roles. Your sympathetic nervous system carries signals that alert your body's systems, and your parasympathetic nervous system carries signals that return those systems to their standard activity levels. Your sympathetic nervous system takes the lead when your safety and survival are at risk, but that system's actions can strain body systems when it's active for too long. Because these two systems offset each other, they help maintain balance in your body."[13]

Our brains take in information that signals when our body needs to activate the sympathetic nervous system. First, the amygdala, or the emotional center of our brain, receives the signal. When it experiences a moment of danger, it signals the hypothalamus, which then fires off and tells the sympathetic nervous system to release all the stress hormones. This is our fight/flight/freeze/fawn response.

After times of stress and trauma triggers, it's essential to signal the parasympathetic system to do its work. To calm the body down. To return to rest. Like in the car rider line, it's trying to signal you to get in park, settle in, and take the foot off the gas. How and what do we do to get our parasympathetic systems working after times of stress and trauma?

Move Your Body

One of the first things I would tell you about running a marathon is something I wish I'd done more of. You must move your body. It doesn't help just to put on the tennis shoes, even if they are the nicest running shoes in the world. And no matter how cute your Lululemon outfit is (I own one thing from that store, and that's because I won a gift card at my gym!), you won't be able to finish the race if you don't move.

Putting in the miles, putting your foot one step in front of the other, is what gets you to the finish line. Healing from trauma is a marathon, not a sprint, and will take one baby step after another. And part of that can be literal steps. Moving. Exercising. Going for that walk or that hike. This is a great way to begin to teach your brain and body to get the parasympathetic nervous system to do the work of calming your nervous system down.

> Healing from trauma is a marathon, not a sprint, and will take one baby step after another.

It sounds way too simple. But the good news is, it's free! My challenge to you: write down ways you'd like to move. Maybe it's yoga, perhaps it's a walk, or maybe it's a long trail hike. Maybe you'd like to bicycle, go to a gym class, or lift weights. Whatever it is, it's essential to do it. This will help you get out of the fight, flight, freeze, or fawn mode.

Both when I was being trained as a yoga teacher and during my trauma counseling training, we were assigned to read the book *The Body Keeps the Score*. In yoga teacher training, they taught us that trauma is often stored in the hips. While this is not clinically proven, it is true that when the fight/flight/freeze/fawn response is activated and our cortisol levels rise, we tend to tighten the muscles there to prepare for action. Our bodies hold tension in the hips, shoulders and neck.

I noticed when I started doing yoga classes, we often ended the class with a twist lying on our backs to stretch our hips. I'm not a person who typically cries, but frequently when I would do that pose, I'd find tears spontaneously rolling down my cheeks. Doing the movement in yoga released something in my body, which began to release emotions stored in my mind. This is the power of movement.

In the next chapter, we'll move more specifically into some action steps we can take based on your typical stress response style. Remember, while we may have one typical stress and trauma response, we will probably experience them all at one time or another. Looking at each response style and finding ways to lower the stress response can be helpful.

Just a note

I wanted to add a note here for you before going into some of the more practical tips and techniques. As I've mentioned before in this book, I don't want to slap a Bible verse on your pain. This is a tricky balancing act for me because, as a believer in Jesus and the power of His Word and the presence of the Holy Spirit, I am so thankful for how He's comforted me. Helped me. Given me encouragement through the Word. But I also recognize it's complicated and painful when trauma and hard things are involved in our stories.

It isn't very easy because it comes with questions. Where's God? What is He doing? Is He safe? And I want to reiterate to you that these are normal questions, and I believe we can run to God and pour out our whole hearts, even our anger, to Him. I love how the Psalms are examples of this. Psalm 22:1, for example, opens with the line, "My God, my God, why have you forsaken me?" Jesus said these exact words when He was dying an excruciating death on the cross. He understands lament and powerful questions from the heart.

You're not failing. You're lamenting. And it's holy.

I've found the presence of God to be a safe place, but I want you to know you're welcome here even if you haven't found that to be true.

Heart Work: From Traffic Cop Chaos to Coffee Shop Calm

You made it through the math problems. You survived the marathon (even if you maybe walked . . . a lot of it). You've learned that your brain and body aren't trying to sabotage you—they're trying to *save* you, even if that looks like sweating through school pickup or freezing mid-earthquake during a TikTok scroll.

Now it's time to help your brain and body know you're safe again.

Let's make this practical, with grace and baby steps.

1. Your Inner Traffic Cop

Your nervous system has two "traffic cops" giving signals:

Sympathetic = go, go, go! (fight, flight, freeze, fawn)

Parasympathetic = slow down, breathe, rest

PROMPT: Think back to a recent moment when your body was in full-on "go" mode. What did your inner traffic cop feel like?

"In that moment, I felt my body trying to _____.
I now realize that was my _____ nervous system at work."

Now ask:

"What signal might help me slow down or stop next time?"

_____

_____

_____

2. Move Like It Matters (Because It Does)

Healing from trauma isn't a sprint—it's a marathon. And marathons require movement. Not fancy gear or winning medals. Just . . . movement.

PROMPT: List three types of movement you enjoy *(or at least tolerate):*

1.

2.

3.

Commit to trying one of them this week—not to fix anything, but to *remind your body it's safe to move again.*

3. My Body Keeps the Score—So I'll Listen

Whether it's yoga, hiking, dancing in your kitchen, or shaking out your limbs after a hard day, your body is talking.

Reflection: What's a part of your body where you often feel stress, pain, or tension?

"When I'm stressed, I feel it in my _____ _____."
"What might my body be trying to tell me?"

Now consider: How can I care for that area more gently this week?

4. Lower the Volume on Fight Mode

Here's your cheat sheet for when the inner fighter wakes up swinging:

Fight Response Soothers:

- 🌿 Deep breathing (4 count in / 4 count hold / 4 count out)
- 🌿 Walking away with intention
- 🌿 Progressive muscle relaxation
- 🌿 Journaling your unedited feelings
- 🌿 Prayer or meditation
- 🌿 Visualization of a safe place
- 🌿 Speaking truth to yourself gently
- 🌿 Noticing without judging

TRY THIS RIGHT NOW: Take three deep breaths. On each exhale, say silently or aloud: "I'm safe now."

Then write: "The next time I feel like a volcano about to erupt, I will try _____ first."

5. God, Trauma & Lament

If you've wrestled with questions like:

- 🌿 "Where were You, God?"
- 🌿 "Why did this happen?"
- 🌿 "Can I trust You again?"

You're not failing. You're *lamenting*. And it's holy.

PROMPT: What's a question, fear, or frustration you want to bring honestly before God right now?

Write it raw. Write it real. Then follow it with this:

"I don't have all the answers, but I'm still here. Still breathing. Still hoping You're good."

6. Safe Might Not Feel Safe—But God Still Is

PROMPT: Write a prayer or declaration for your journey. Something like:

"God, I don't always feel safe. But I want to believe You're good."

"Even when my body screams, You whisper peace."

"Help me know it's okay to take the next right step."

You're not alone. You're not behind. You're rebuilding—one breath, one stretch, one grounding sip of coffee at a time.

In the next chapter, we'll dive into action steps tailored to your stress response style. For now, celebrate that you're noticing. That you're moving. That you're still in the race.

And that's a really big deal.

CHAPTER 8

BABY STEPS, BREATHWORK, AND BLASTS OF COLD

I love pickleball, as does most of the world right now. I don't play much anymore, because the people I was playing with have decided they want to get as good as Olympians (*keep in mind that pickleball isn't even an Olympic sport!*) and I've decided I'm okay with just staying mediocre. One of the things I've noticed about pickleball is that the serve is essential. (*And unfortunately, that's one of my most mediocre moves, especially when we're at game point. I feel bad for my teammates because I ALWAYS crumble under pressure.*) But the game isn't just about the serve. There's a moment when "serving no longer serves you!" You must move forward on the court and start hitting the ball back and forth.

The fight, flight, freeze, or fawn response is meant to serve you in the moment, to help you survive. However, we don't want to stay stuck in this highly activated mode. There's a point where you must begin to move forward so that your body doesn't stay stuck in that heightened state of stress and trauma. In this chapter, I'll offer some practical tools and ideas to help you move forward.

These action step ideas are just starting points for you. You'll find that some work better for you than others. This isn't an exhaustive list; the few short paragraphs on each are meant to give you tiny baby steps to healing. I encourage you to find books or counselors to help you if you want to learn more about any particular area. When I teach about trauma care, I teach in different areas, from huts in third-world countries with few resources to churches in America with access to everything. I've found trauma survivors want small, actionable steps to find healing, so I wanted to share these action steps with you and encourage you to learn more about the ones that seem to serve you best.

Breathing

When you experience a trauma trigger, your heart rate and cortisol levels increase. Because of this, it's essential to decrease your heart rate. You can do this by the act of breathing. I love this because it is free and can be done anywhere.

There are so many different types of breathwork. I encourage you to do a simple Google search on breathing. One to practice first is closing your eyes. *(Only as long as you feel safe to do so; if not feel free to leave them open!)* Inhale to the count of four, then hold for the count of four, then exhale for the count of four. This is called box breathing, and you can also visualize drawing a box as you do this. Do this for as many rounds as you can. Your heart rate will decrease, and your blood pressure will stabilize.

You can also focus on making the exhale longer or more pronounced. This will activate the parasympathetic nervous system. It can be fun to make this exhale loud! We learned a breathing technique in yoga teacher training called lion's breath. It feels ridiculous, but it's a fun way to get out a big exhale. You take a deep breath, hold your breath with your mouth almost like you have a bubble inside, then release by sticking out your tongue and making a loud exhale noise. Not only will you get a good exhale, but it may also help you as you get a good laugh.

This brings back a fun memory that must be shared. When I lived in Nepal, I traveled to Calcutta, India. I didn't realize they wouldn't take Nepalese rupees (the Nepalese form of cash) there, so when I got to the airport late at night, I had no money to get a taxi. A young girl in line beside me said she was happy to share a cab with me and that we could go together to the YMCA hostel where we would stay.

I found out she was traveling with the Travel Channel to do a documentary on India. She asked if I would join her the next day for part of their documentary to film a so-called laughing club in the park. Call something a laughing club and I'm IN! I will never forget it. The people take the laughing club very seriously. They had a leader in the middle of the circle who would say, "Ha," and they would repeat it back. Then he would say "Ha-ha," and they would repeat it back, and so on. Eventually, one by one, they would all start hysterically laughing. I laughed the whole time! Maybe you should start your own laughing club!

As a serious note, if you find yourself in the frozen mode of trauma response, it's crucial to take some long, deep breaths. People who are frozen tend to hold their breath without even realizing it. Instead, take two quick inhales and a much longer exhale to remind you not to hold your breath.

Progressive Muscle Relaxation

Progressive muscle relaxation can be a great tool to help your body release some of the stress hormones it carries. This tool enables you to bring awareness to what's happening in your body and can help you regain a sense of control. Trauma makes us feel out of control, so this is a good way to help the body begin to feel safe again.

In progressive muscle relaxation, you can choose to start up or down. I usually pick down because my feet are the part of me I often notice the most, *(don't make fun of my "old lady" foot problems like a bunion and plantar fasciitis!)* but you can start at your head and go down.

Pick a muscle group and tighten it as much as you can.

Right now, I'm starting with my toes. I curl them tight *(I have toes that are as long as fingers, which comes in handy sometimes!)* and hold for about 5–10 seconds, then release. That release feels so good! Then I go to my calves *(which happen to be very tight from kettlebell class today, where the instructor had us do an ungodly amount of calf raises while holding a way-too-big kettlebell)* and tighten them and hold for those 5–10 seconds and release. Pick major muscle groups and go all the way up to your eyeballs. Feel free to get creative.

This simple practice helps connect you back to your body. The relaxation that comes with releasing the tension helps tell your body it's safe to relax. Just like breathing, it helps get that parasympathetic nervous system working like you want it to and can help you regain a sense of control.

Walk Away

Sometimes your fight mode has been activated because you're in a fight with someone. Relationship trauma or stress can raise cortisol and activate the sympathetic nervous system, and if you are in fight mode, sometimes it's best just to walk away and take a break from the conversation. Sometimes we must tell the person we need to walk away and revisit the discussion at a different time when we feel more regulated. When you walk away, this may be a good time to walk and physically move your body.

If you're a fawn *(why does it feel so weird to type that? I always picture a cute baby deer)*, your form of walking away may need to be learning to practice the art of saying no. Goodness! For such a small, easy word to spell, it can be hard for all of us to say no. Especially for the fawn. Learning to set boundaries and say no is an essential piece of healing for the fawn.

If you are a fawner, a good question is: "Am I responding to this situation in this way because I'm trying to establish safety by pleasing them? Why am I taking this action?" If you respond this way to find safety as a people pleaser, learning to set boundaries and say no will help you not stay stuck in fawn survival mode.

Meditation and Prayer

Meditation involves being still and quiet, breathing, and taking time to pause. Maybe you're like me; this isn't your regular soul exercise. Or perhaps you love being still and quiet, pausing in the space of time *(all the introverts among us say AMEN!)*. In which-ever direction you fall, meditation can be a beneficial practice for those who have been impacted by trauma. The stillness helps regulate the nervous system. It reminds you that you're safe and connected with the present moment. It can help shrink the part of your brain that bends towards fear and create new neural pathways for healing.

As a Christian, I find combining meditation and prayer a helpful spiritual and emotional practice. After the stillness of meditation, I pour out my heart in prayer. Another helpful prac-tice is picking a scripture verse to focus on during meditation. One of my favorites is Isaiah 26:3: "You keep him in perfect peace whose mind is stayed on you." I close my eyes, breathe in, and say to myself, "He will keep me in perfect peace", and then, as I breathe out, "As my mind is stayed on you." This is how I do it; feel free to make this practice your own. *(As a note, you do not have to add the scripture and prayer part to meditation; these are just ways that I've incorporated spiritual practices.)*

I do want to make you aware that mediation can be triggering in the beginning, depending on what type of trauma has impacted your life. If you find it causes more anxiety, start slow. Set a timer for 1–3 minutes. Be mindful of what is going on in your brain and body. Scan your body to see how it feels in the moment and where you find tension. Notice where your feet are, what you're touching, etc. You may need to start with your eyes open instead of closed. Or try moving while you do it—walking, yoga, etc. Also, if your thoughts feel too much for you at the time, you could listen to soothing sounds or music.

Visualization is a practice you could use either with meditation or on its own. In visualization, you imagine a place that feels safe and comforting. This can be a place you've been to, an imaginary place, or an image of a place. You can get as detailed as you want with this image. When your body begins to feel dysregulated or your stress hormones are racing, take a moment to visualize that safe image. Imagining the details of the place, such as what you would see, feel, and hear there, will help bring a richer experience to your visualization. The more often you return to this safe place in your mind, the more grounding it becomes. Therapists often use this technique in their office when clients need to regulate their brain and body from a trauma response.

Journaling

I still remember my first diary. It was rose-scented and had a little key. I don't know what I wrote in it at the ripe old age of eight. Maybe something like "Dear diary, I am sorry I was mean to my twin sister again," or "I got in trouble at school for talking AGAIN." I have stacks and stacks of journals I hope someone burns upon my death, because I feel like it would be slightly embarrassing to have them out there for the world to see.

I also used my journals to write out prayers, so that's part of why I keep them. It's so amazing to go back and read what I was pouring out from my heart to God in my journal and then think about how He answered. The high school and college ones are just plain fun. To remember the crush on that boy and the dumb things I did, including stealing a pair of his socks at the skating rink one day and keeping it in my hope chest in case we had a future marriage. *(I have since gotten rid of those white crew socks!)*

Journaling can be a great practice to help you as you process through trauma and trauma triggers. I encourage you to write in your journal without editing your thoughts or emotions. A helpful journal prompt could be: Right now, if I were allowed to feel, I would feel _____.

A 2018 study published in JMIR Mental Health found that journaling for fifteen minutes three days a week was enough to lower blood pressure and increase feelings of well-being. These benefits are linked to reduced levels of cortisol—often called the "stress hormone"—in the body. Remarkably, participants in the study showed a 19% reduction in cortisol levels after just one month of a regular journaling practice.14

Something you can pair with journaling is cognitive behavioral work. Cognitive behavioral work looks at how our thinking impacts our feelings and actions, and it emphasizes the importance of examining what we're thinking and how that can link to our actions and feelings. If you're an American reader and looking for a counselor who works from a cognitive behavioral framework, you can look in your area on psychologytoday.com and it should list what modality different counselors use. If you're feeling triggered, ask yourself: Is this feeling based on a current threat or memory? What was happening in your space before, after and during the trigger? What were you thinking, feeling, and observing? What is one thing that gives me hope right now? Is this a fact or a fear? What need or emotion might be underneath this thought?

Stress Release Plan

Everyone is different in the ways in which they release their stress. For some, a good run is the way they're able to release stress. For others, simply reading that sentence reminded you of gym class and having to do the dreaded fitness test with the one-mile run, made you *feel* stressed just thinking about it.

Some love cooking or baking. Sourdough baking is all the rage, at least on Instagram. For some of you, the idea of baking bread makes all your stresses go away. For others, reading that you must keep the starter alive makes you want to die a little inside.

I encourage you to make a stress release plan so that you can be intentional about having a list of ideas when you're feeling overwhelmed or triggered by trauma. I recognize that it doesn't make the stress disappear, but it can be an invaluable tool when you cannot think of what to do.

Does taking a warm bath help? Taking a walk with a friend? Going to a group fitness class? How would you answer the question, "What makes you come alive?" I always asked my counseling clients this question because they were often so stressed out that they had no idea anymore. Making a self-care list or a stress release plan is a way to turn good intentions to build serotonin (the brain's happy chemicals) into action.

Cold plunging has become very trendy. I'm not one to always want to jump on the trends, but I'll tell you that the more I studied the benefits of cold plunging, the more I decided to give it a try.

When I returned from the earthquake in Turkey, I was stressed out, traumatized, and stuck in burnout both from ministry and releasing my first traditionally published book. One of the things I wrote on my self-care/stress release plan was to try cold plunging. I love extremes, so I also love a good sweat-everything-out-in-your-body sauna experience. I found a place downtown where you can rent a sauna for an hour, go from the sauna to a cold plunge pool, and return to the sauna.

It took quite a lot to convince me to plunge deep inside that cold water *(I wanted to settle with just putting my big toe in—surely that would count for something, right?)* But I did it. Once I caught my breath, I tried to slow my breathing without letting everyone in the building know I was in the cold plunge pool. Once I got out of the pool, wrapped a warm towel around my body, I immediately noticed that it had indeed relaxed me.

What exactly happens when you take a cold plunge? The vagus nerve, which helps your body move from the fight/flight/freeze/fawn survival mode into "rest mode," is activated quickly in cold water. The more you cold plunge, the more it exercises the vagus nerve, slowing your heart rate and regulating everything from digestion to emotions. If you're up for it, give it a try. *(I should remind you that I am not a doctor, although I wanted to be one until I took Biology 101 in college and decided it wasn't for me. So please don't take this as medical advice, and feel free to consult with your medical doctor to ensure this is a good idea for you and your body.)*

Grounding

It's been one of those Tennessee spring weather weeks where the sun will be blazing through the clouds, and then suddenly, when you least expect it, the sky will be pouring sheets of rain. I took my shoes off during a respite between rainstorms and stood barefoot on the soggy, wet ground. I knew my feet would get dirty, but I also knew that writing a book on trauma can be stressful, so I needed to get my feet on the ground in the middle of my writing.

This is one of the grounding techniques you can use. It's pretty simple—put your feet on the ground and notice it. Now, maybe you're thinking what I used to think. Does this even help? Why would we waste our time putting our bare feet on the ground? Like the other action steps in this chapter, grounding helps bring your body and brain to the present moment. Anxiety is future-focused, and trauma can cause flashbacks to your past, so grounding is a way to bring your brain and body to the present moment. It regulates the nervous system, activating the prefrontal cortex, which can tend to shut down after periods of trauma. It can help those who dissociate due to their trauma or feel numb and shut down. It regulates you emotionally. When you ground, it doesn't have to be outside; you can also do it on a floor, paying attention to where your feet are planted. Wiggle your toes. Feel the pressure of the floor or ground and remind your body that you're safe in that moment.

There are other physical ways you can practice grounding. As mentioned before, cold water helps activate the vagus nerve, so you can splash your face with cold water, or hold a couple of ice cubes. In fact, you can hold any object in your hand. For example, hold a smooth rock. Rub your hands on the rock. Notice how it feels in the palm of your hand. Anything with texture will work great. It can be a soft blanket, a piece of clay that you knead in your hand, or something rough that you rub your hands over. You could create a grounding box to hold these things that help you practice grounding. Your box may contain a smooth stone, sour candy, or an essential oil. Keep the grounding box handy and use it whenever you feel triggered by your trauma.

Other soothing things can help you with grounding. Find a soothing scent of essential oil, lotion, or facewash and use that to help bring you back to the present moment, activating your parasympathetic nervous system. You can also establish a safe place in your home or space that feels grounding to you. Get some cozy blankets, a beautiful piece of artwork, a comfy chair for your safe space—anything that makes you feel emotionally and physically safe and go to that space when you experience a trauma trigger.

There's also the 5-4-3-2-1 method. When you find yourself feeling overwhelmed, dysregulated, or even having a panic attack, you can use this method. This will help your brain be connected to the present moment.

5-4-3-2-1 METHOD
(Help your brain be connected to the moment.)

Name **5 things** you can see in the moment.

What are **4 things** you can feel around you?

What are **3 things** you can hear?

What are **2 things** you can smell?

What is **1 thing** you can taste?

You can also use mental grounding—think of it like a game. You can count backwards by tens, do multiplication facts, count by twos. Get as creative as you want. I'm probably going to be joining you in using math facts as my grounding techniques. Remember what I said about calculus class?

You can repeat a mantra over and over in your heart. Tell yourself, "I am safe. I am calm. I am strong. I am capable." Remind yourself, "God loves me. God is with me." Add a Bible verse to it, such as Psalm 27:1a, "The Lord is my light and salvation whom shall I fear?" Repeat these phrases repeatedly until they stick.

Look around and describe your environment. "The chair is brown leather. The air is cold. I hear rain outside. The kitchen table is square, long and has scratches in the top of it." Be specific. You can say these observations out loud, write them down, or tell a friend. This can be especially helpful when trying to come out of a moment of panic.

> Tell yourself, "I am safe. I am calm. I am strong. I am capable."

As a note, if you're experiencing a trauma flashback, one of the best things you can do to bring you into the present moment is engage the five senses. I found this to be very helpful for me after my car accident. I hydroplaned six times on the interstate before hitting another car head-on going 70 mph. I remember every spin of the car, the sounds, the look of hitting the other car, and the concrete barrier. I've had frequent flashbacks while driving, which isn't safe or ideal. My counselor reminded me of the power of using the five senses when having a flashback. The minute one would start I would open the window to feel the air on my face. I'd always have either cold water or hot coffee in the car so that I could not only taste it but feel it. I kept sour candy close by to wake up my taste buds. I had a song I'd play repeatedly in the car whenever I had a flashback. ("Back to Life" by Bethel if you're curious.) If you find yourself having flashbacks of your traumatic event, engaging your senses will help you come back to the present moment.

Humming and singing are also very good for activating the vagus nerve and the parasympathetic nervous system so feel free to join Buddy the Elf from the movie *Elf* by belting out those tunes. He proclaimed, "I am singing. I am in a store, and I am singing!"[15] Sing, hum, loud and proud. It doesn't have to be on key or tuned just right to stimulate your vagus nerve.

Different grounding techniques work for different people. You may need a gentle approach like a soft blanket or holding a smooth stone. I need stronger forms of sensory input, so I love the cold plunge, the ice holding, the sweating it out in a hot sauna, the spicy food. Find what works for you. You don't have to try all the action steps in this chapter at once, just try out a few and see what works for you. These tools can help you feel like you can slowly regain some sort of safety as you adjust to your new normal of life after trauma.

Heart Work: When Serving No Longer Serves You

You made it to the chapter where we put some powerful tools in your healing backpack. This isn't a "fix your trauma in five easy steps" plan. It's more like a "try what feels gentle today and maybe again tomorrow" invitation. This *Heart Work* gives you some space to experiment, with grace.

Ready to stop standing frozen at the serve line and move back onto the court?

1. What's Your "Serve" That No Longer Serves?

PROMPT: What's something you've been doing in survival mode (a coping mechanism, habit, or mindset) that may have served you during trauma but is now keeping you stuck?

"At the time, _____ helped me survive."

"Now, I think it might be time to gently let go of _____

_____."

For example: "At the time, being a people pleaser and saying yes to anything helped me survive. Now, I think it might be time to gently let go of always having to please everyone and do everything as my response.

2. Your Nervous System: More Than Just Nerves

PROMPT: Write a thank–you note to your nervous system.

Yes, really. Talk to it like it's a friend who got you out of danger, but maybe now needs a nap and a warm blanket.

"Dear Nervous System, I see you trying to protect me. Thank you for _____ .

I'm learning now that it's okay to be safe again. Let's try _____ together."

_____

_____

_____

_____

3. Take a Breath—Seriously.

Try one of these today:

- ❧ Box Breathing: 4 count in / 4 count hold / 4 count out / 4 count hold
- ❧ Double Exhale: Two quick breaths in, one long exhale
- ❧ Lion's Breath: Deep breath in, stick out your tongue, exhale loudly, and maybe giggle

REFLECTION:

"Which breath made me feel the most grounded today?"

"Where in my body did I notice the shift?"

_____

_____

_____

_____

4. Get Physical

Try Progressive Muscle Relaxation.

Pick one set of muscles—feet, fists, shoulders. Tighten for 5–10 seconds. Release. Repeat.

Then journal:

"After tensing and releasing _____ , I noticed _____."

_____

_____

_____

_____

5. Journal Without Editing

Set a timer for five minutes. Don't edit. Don't overthink. Just write.

- "Right now, I feel _____ because _____."
- "I wish people knew _____ about what I've been through."
- "If I were allowed to feel anything today, I would feel _____."

_____

_____

_____

_____

_____

6. Get Grounded

TRY THIS: What are five things you can do, even right now, to ground yourself in the present moment?

Describe your personal grounding toolkit:

1.   Something I can touch: _____

2.   Something I can see: _____

3.   Something I can smell/taste: _____

4.   Something I can say: _____

5.   A breath pattern I can try: _____

7. Build Your Grounding Box

What helps you come back to the moment?

Start your box with:

- 1 object to touch (soft blanket, smooth stone)
- 1 thing to taste (sour candy, mint gum)
- 1 thing to smell (essential oil, lotion)
- 1 mantra or verse (Psalm 27:1, "I am safe.")

Add one more thing this week.

8. Brave the Cold (or at Least a Splash)

Try one of these:

- Splash cold water on your face
- Hold ice in your hand
- Take a cold shower or . . . cold plunge if you're brave

JOURNAL PROMPT:

"When I did the cold _____, I felt _____ .
What surprised me most was _____ ."

_____

_____

_____

_____

9. Meditate and Pray (Yes, Even If You Fidget)

Pick one practice to try this week:

- Meditate for three minutes, focusing on your breath
- Repeat a verse like Isaiah 26:3
- Visualize a safe place (real or imaginary) and describe it in detail
- Sit with your questions and let them breathe

FINISH THIS SENTENCE: "God, today I need you to remind me that _____ ."

10. Make Your Stress Release Plan

List three go-to ways to release stress *that work for you.*

1.

2.

3.

Write them on a sticky note. Put it where your eyeballs will see it.

11. Sing Like Buddy the Elf

Because humming and singing activate your vagus nerve and help you regulate. *(Yes, even if it's off-key.)*

"Today, I will sing/hum this song: _____ "

"Music that grounds me when I feel shaky: _____ "

Trauma may have knocked you down. But each tool in this chapter is like tying your shoes again, standing up, and walking toward something new—even if it's just one shaky step at a time.

You don't have to try everything at once.

Pick one. Start there. And know you're already doing the brave work of coming back to life.

CHAPTER 9

YOUR STORY DESERVES TO BREATHE

(EVEN IF YOU'RE STILL IN THE RUBBLE)

This chapter is about how to tell your story, lean on others, and ask for help. If you feel help is hard to find, I wrote this book with you in mind, all the while praying that you wouldn't feel alone in your suffering anymore.

I'm going to type out a prayer I'm praying over you right now:

God, I pray for the one reading these words. I pray you will send someone to walk beside and with them in whatever ways they feel alone right now. I thank you for your presence with them. I pray peace over them. I pray encouragement for them. And I pray strength for their journey of healing and release. In Jesus' name, Amen.

It's Important to Tell Your Story

There's something about telling our stories that's freeing. This is the part of the book where I want to encourage you to lean on others. You can learn how to tell your story so that it doesn't have to stay only inside you.

I will never forget meeting Lolance on my fifth trip to Haiti. Our team led a kids' camp for around 600 kids a day *(talk about a room full of energy!)* and a special needs camp for adults with differing abilities in the afternoon. There was something that drew me to Lolance when her mom brought her to the special needs camp that first day. I kept being drawn to spend time with her.

We did arts and crafts together. I danced with her, played silly games with her, and sat with her. All the while, she did not speak, smile, or interact at all. She simply sat there with us. As the week progressed, I learned more about Lolance's story.

She was working an office job on January 12, 2010, when one of the deadliest earthquakes in history occurred. Because she was at work and separated from her husband and two children, she began to panic and tried to get to her family as soon as the ground started shaking.

She was never able to find her husband or children. They perished in the rubble that day. Lolance didn't have the resources to process this trauma, so as the days went by, she began to lose her ability to function. The shock and trauma caused her to lose her ability to speak and process, even the ability to feed herself or take care of her own hygiene needs.

At the end of that week, one of the greatest joys in my life happened; I was able to make Lolance smile. She hadn't smiled in over eight years or even spoken a word. She mouthed a few words to me, and I don't think my heart has ever been the same.

I became passionate about helping people process their trauma stories and learn to tell their stories, so they don't have to experience what Lolance had to walk through.

As I've traveled elsewhere for trauma care after natural disasters, one of the things we focus on is the group debriefing time. It is a time for people to share their stories, to release them. When I prepare people for the debriefing, I share the example of a bottle of Coke. What happens if you shake a bottle of Coke? Pressure builds up. What happens if you suddenly open the bottle? The Coke will explode. However, if you carefully open it and let the air escape slowly, safely, the pressure inside the bottle is relieved.

This is what happens when you tell your story. The pressure inside you from holding onto your experiences can be slowly relieved. It's important to find someone safe to tell your story to. The best-case scenario is finding a trained counselor. But if that isn't available to you or you don't have the resources to afford a counselor, I want to give you some other ways to tell your story.

When I do the debriefing, after the Coke bottle illustration, I ask the audience, "How many ears do we have?' They tell me two. Then I will say, "How many mouths do we have?" They usually chuckle and say one. I then point out how God gave us two ears and one mouth, and we should remember that it's essential when someone is sharing their trauma story with us that we listen instead of talk.

The first debriefing experience I had was after my time in Nepal. I lived there for two years, and when I came back, my graduate school professor asked if her class could practice doing a group debrief with me about my time there. I remember walking into the room to a circle of chairs and eight people, plus my professor. She asked a simple guiding question to begin the debrief, telling me to share anything I wanted to about my time in Nepal. Those in the circle were instructed not to talk, but to listen and ask the occasional guiding question. I was so surprised by what came out as I was allowed to tell my story for two hours, while being truly heard. It provided healing I didn't even realize I needed. It's so easy for all of us to want to go into fix-it mode when someone is telling us their hard stories because it's human nature to want to fix things and make them better. But in the case of telling your trauma story, that isn't helpful. What you need is to release your story and pour it into a safe container.

How to Tell Your Story

When leading group or individual debriefs, I teach people to share their story in a way that helps their brain to process safely. The first thing to do is talk about the event by sharing what you were experiencing with your senses during the event. What did you see with your eyes, feel, smell, hear, etc.? Sharing what your senses experienced first, helps ground you and helps your brain process the story. Then move from there to sharing what you were thinking during the event. What was going through your mind as you experienced your trauma, or series of traumas? After sharing this, share what you were feeling.

Share what you remember with your five senses.

Share what you were thinking.

Share what you were feeling.

If at any point you find yourself getting triggered or emotionally and physically flooded when telling your trauma story, make sure to stop, pause, and practice one of the grounding tech- niques we mentioned in the previous chapter. After your body becomes more regulated, you can begin sharing again. Or if you find it hard to stay regulated, or experience a flashback, it may be best to take this slowly and pause the story to share more at another time when you feel more grounded.

If you cannot find someone to listen to your trauma story, you may discover journaling as a helpful release as well. Follow the same pattern by writing what you were experiencing with your senses, what you were thinking during the traumatic event, and what you were feeling.

Telling your story isn't a magic wand; it's just one of the steps in your healing journey. However, there is something so powerful about the release as you share and shape the story.

There is hope for healing!

Finding a Counselor

As mentioned in these pages, I encourage you to find a trained counselor when that resource is available. Some of the evidence-based practices counselors may have specific training in that are shown to help those dealing with trauma can include:

EMDR: Eye Movement Desensitization and Reprocessing

Brain Mapping

Trauma-Focused CBT

Acceptance and Commitment Therapy

Professionals are constantly learning more about the science of trauma and its impact on brain and body health and finding more ways to help empower those who've been impacted by trauma to gain healing. There is hope for healing!

What If?

Friend, I want to acknowledge something hard. Some of you are still in trauma. You aren't healing from trauma in the past; you are dealing with trauma in your present life. I couldn't finish this chapter without acknowledging that. I recently sat with a circle of amazing Haitian women who had to escape unimaginable atrocities in Haiti. There's no legal safe place for them to live, so they had to deal with traumas like hiding in the bushes with their children. I was teaching a trauma training to women who were still living in trauma.

The same is true for when I've worked in countries at war. I'll never forget doing a trauma debriefing when we had to run and take cover because the air raid sirens were going off to alert us of another missile attack. Their trauma was ongoing.

If you're still in the trauma and there's no way out, I want you to know that I see you here. You are brave! I want to encourage you to do what you can. Keep practicing these baby steps of healing over and over as you're able, even amid the trauma.

Will it stop the bombs from falling or the trauma from occurring? Unfortunately, no. But it can help you feel a small sense of control in a time that feels out of control.

You've made it to this chapter, which means you're doing the work, and I want to pause to say how deeply proud I am of you. This chapter was about sharing your story, not because you have to, but because something beautiful happens when we let what's been bottled up inside finally have space to breathe.

Here's your invitation to release a little pressure from the Coke bottle. Slowly. Gently. No explosion necessary.

> Something beautiful happens when we let what's been bottled up inside finally have space to breathe.

1. The Five Senses Storytelling Prompt

Think of a moment in your life that holds pain—maybe a big moment or a quiet ache. You don't have to choose the most significant trauma. Just pick what your heart is willing to hold right now. Using the framework below, write freely without editing yourself:

- What did you see?
- What did you hear?
- What did you smell?
- What did you feel (touch or sensation)?
- What did you taste?

Now go deeper:

- 🌿 What were you thinking during that moment?
- 🌿 What were you feeling emotionally?

If at any point you start to feel flooded, pause. Breathe. Try a grounding technique—look up from the page, feel your feet on the floor, hold something comforting in your hand, or get that sour candy you hid in the back of the pantry.)

2. Tell Someone Safe

Who is someone in your life you feel might have "two ears and one mouth"—a listener, not a fixer?

Jot their name here: ⎯⎯⎯⎯⎯⎯⎯⎯⎯⎯⎯⎯⎯⎯⎯

If no one comes to mind, that's okay. Write a prayer or letter instead to God, to your future healed self, or even to me *(I promise I'm cheering you on from afar)*.

3. Reclaiming Your Voice

Sometimes trauma steals the microphone from our story. It's your turn to take it back. Complete the sentences below:

🌿 "What I wish someone knew about what I've gone through is . . . "

_____

_____

_____

_____

🌿 "If I could tell my younger self one thing, it would be . . . "

_____

_____

_____

_____

🌿 "One thing I want to believe about my story is . . . "

_____

_____

_____

_____

_____

4. Release and Root

After writing, close your eyes and take a few deep breaths. Picture yourself placing this story somewhere safe—a journal, God's hands, a counselor's office, or a campfire in your mind where it can be held and honored.

Then write:

- 🌿 One word I want to take with me after this: _____

Let this be your reminder: your story matters, and you don't have to carry it alone. Keep writing. Keep sharing. Keep breathing.

You're not too much, not too broken, and not too late to heal.

CHAPTER 10

SPACE TO HOPE AGAIN

I'm fresh off the jet lag of returning from a trip back to Turkey. *(Did I mention that whenever I cross a time zone, even if it's one, I can use jet lag as an excuse for anything? My friends know that if I say or do something that doesn't make sense— for at least a month—JET LAG!)*

I travel all the time, but this felt like one of my most significant trips. I returned to the rubble. To the place where I'd seen the most trauma of my life and experienced my own trauma. I went back to Turkey. The place where the idea for finding hope beneath the rubble was born.

> Where you've been impacts where you're going.

I returned two years to the week of when the large earthquake had occurred. I had so many feelings as I got on the plane to return to the place where I'd seen the most despair, destruction, and rubble of my life. This was the place where I'd seen trauma up close and personal as we experienced, together, the second earthquake rumbling the ground.

As I landed and began my journey into the city, I still saw some rubble. But I also saw a city being rebuilt. Some things were the same, some still in process, and some completely new and different. I saw people who'd found the space to hope again walking in their new normal.

I'm praying that for you as you come to this last chapter of the book. Trauma takes time to heal, so I realize there may be things that still feel just the same as when you experienced your trauma or traumas. Some things are in the process of rebuilding. And some things are completely new and different.

Reflecting Back

I don't need to tell you that our world today is crazy fast-paced. It can be easy to just want to move on. Move forward. I know I love a good goal, a good dream, a vision for what's to come, and a moving forward plan. And when I picture you, the reader, I picture you moving forward into hope. Taking those baby steps that slowly, but surely, bring big healing.

I know it's easy to want to quick speed look ahead, move forward, not look back. But I do want you to take a moment as you're finishing this book to reflect back. Because where you've been impacts where you're going.

Let me remind you of our acrostic.

RUBBLE

Rebuilding is Possible

Understand Trauma and Its Effects

Brain

Body

Leaning into Others and how to ask for help

Experience Hope

Experience Hope

Together, we started with the reminder that rebuilding is possible. Sometimes we need someone to tell us that, to hold hope for us, and to stand with us on the holy ground of suffering as we ask, "Will I ever feel normal again?'

Then we learned what was normal as we started to grasp and understand trauma and its effects. You may need to return to those chapters as you become a noticer. Noticing when you experience a trigger. Reminding yourself that you're normal.

Even on my recent trip back to Turkey, I had to remind myself of some typical effects of trauma. For example, the earthquake I was in happened at night, so I found myself extra jumpy and struggling to sleep. *(This was either an effect of trauma or could have been the eighteen cups of Turkish coffee I had in a day, because the people are so hospitable and want to serve you well!)* I had to practice some of my brain and body tools to calm my body down, so it was ready to sleep. So, here's your permission slip to go back to those pages to revisit the tips and techniques often as you begin to recognize when you may have entered fight, flight, freeze, or fawn mode.

I hope you learned to tell your story safely to safe people. To lean into others. And I'm expectant for you as you continue to experience hope beneath the rubble.

Rebuilding

In high school, I loved going on summer mission trips. We did group mission trips where our youth group would join other youth groups for a week and help homeowners with repainting, light construction, and roofing. I'm unsure why they let groups of inexperienced high schoolers get on a roof and put new roofs on, but they did. Keep in mind these were the same high schoolers who, at night, were having contests on stage as to who could eat the most jalapenos without dying (my sister almost won) and who could say chubby bunny with the most marshmallows in their mouth. I was great for the team morale on these projects, cheering everyone on as they hammered their nails, but I could never seem to hit my own nail. However, I did manage to step on a rusty nail, which lead to a trip to Urgent Care for a tetanus shot.

During my summer mission trips, I learned that in a rebuilding project, you sometimes use brand new materials and sometimes you can build with materials that are old. As you continue to take steps toward healing from your trauma, you'll build your life with some new experiences and new tools, but you'll use some of the "old" experiences too.

The book of Nehemiah in the Bible is all about rebuilding from ruins. We read, "The wall of Jerusalem is broken down, and its gates are destroyed by fire" (Nehemiah 1:3b). The people started to rebuild the walls, and I want to tell you the truth—it was hard work.

I wish rebuilding from trauma were as easy as waving a magic wand. But it's hard. And there will be those who want to oppose your healing. Sometimes people want us to stay the same; for whatever reason, they don't want us to find a new healthy normal. Sometimes people don't want to do the hard work for their own healing, so they want you to stay with them in the ruins of the rubble.

In Nehemiah, we're told of a guy named Sanballat who heard they were rebuilding the wall. In Nehemiah 4, he's described as becoming "greatly enraged." That's a pretty strong word right there—enraged! "What are these feeble Jews doing? Will they restore it for themselves? Will they sacrifice? Will they finish up in a day? Will they review the stones out of the heaps of rubbish, and burned ones at that" (Nehemiah 4:2)?

Some people in your life say those things without saying THOSE things. Why are you dealing with your past trauma? Why do you want to talk about things? Why are you responding in this way? They may not understand your healing journey, and that can be hard. It can make you want to give up. It can make you question whether you wish to continue rebuilding.

That's why I wanted to take some courage from what happens in the book of Nehemiah and share it with you. Nehemiah encouraged the people in this way. "Do not be afraid of them. Remember the Lord, who is great and awesome, and fight for your brothers, your sons, your daughters, your wives, and your homes" (Nehemiah 4:14).

> "Do not be afraid of them. Remember the Lord, who is great and awesome, and fight for your brothers, your sons, your daughters, your wives, and your homes."
> Nehemiah 4:14

Friends, your journey of healing won't just impact you. It will affect those around you. Let me be Nehemiah's voice in your ear. I want you to know that even as I type these words, even if I never meet you, I'm praying for you. I pray you feel strength and courage as you heal. As you continue to do this hard work, I'm asking God to fight for you.

In Nehemiah 6:9, 15–16, we read, "They all wanted to frighten us, thinking, 'Their hands will drop from the work, and it will not be done.' But now, O God, strengthen my hands . . . So the wall was finished on the twenty-fifth day of the month Elul, in fifty-two days. And when all our enemies heard of it, and all the nations around us were afraid, and fell greatly in their esteem, for they perceived that this work had been accomplished with the help of our God."

I cannot tell you that your work of healing will be finished in fifty-two days or in fifty years, but I can tell you that as you take this journey of healing, I believe in God's help to strengthen you.

Sometimes you need to hear this, so I say it loud and proud.

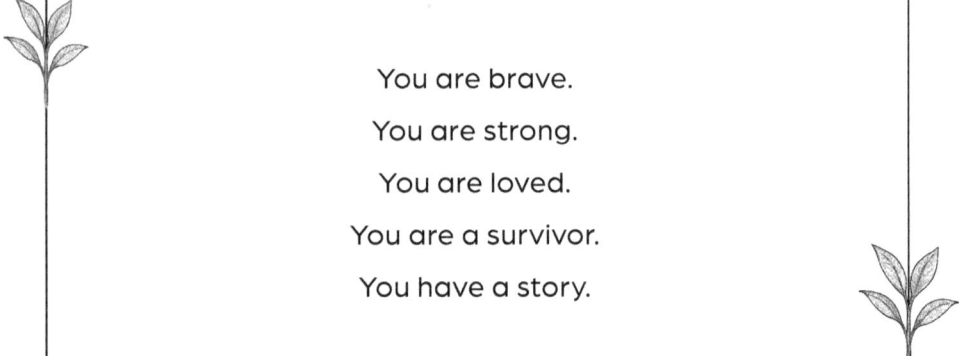

You are brave.

You are strong.

You are loved.

You are a survivor.

You have a story.

And I wish I could send you some of the fancy new, expensive, trendy Dubai chocolate bars everyone is talking about to enjoy while we finish this book, and as you continue in your journey of hope.

The God of Hope

In my book *My Yes is on the Table*, there's a chapter entitled "Giants, Grasshoppers, and a Thread of Hope." In this chapter, I talk about how it can be hard to hope. *"Hope can feel like it is setting us up for a hard fall . . . I have a hard time leaning my weight back on hope. I want to control hope. I want to control my expectations so I can control the outcome or control the disappointments. But when I lean back and risk hope in the character and compassion of God, He can bear the weight of me."*[15]

I've met so many people over the years who've experienced trauma and are scared to hope. I've been the one at times who's experienced trauma and, therefore, been afraid to hope. But I've also learned that when I lean back and risk hope, resting in the character and compassion of God, He can bear the weight of me.

I go to the YMCA three times a week and do a "power hour" workout. Somehow, I end up not looking so powerful, and like maybe I might die before the hour is up. But I keep coming back *(at least on the days my heated blanket and comfy bed don't keep me from getting up)!* We do circuits in small groups of 3–5 people. Today, I did my elevated reverse lunges without holding any extra weight when one of my workout partners encouraged me.

> When I lean back and risk hope, resting in the character and compassion of God, He can bear the weight of me.

"You can do it, Jenn! Grab yourself some weight! You are capable of more than you think."

She held hope in my strength.

In the same circuit, I was supposed to do a thing I believe they call "fallout" using the TRX straps. You can either kneel or stand, while you put your hands in the TRX straps, then lean forward slowly, and come back slowly, using your core.

Typing this, it sounds easy. Doing it feels anything but. I was choosing the kneeling option because I didn't feel like the TRX straps could handle my weight. My trainer believed differently. He came and told me to try the standing "fall out." He reminded me that I worked out every week, was strong, and the straps and core could hold my weight.

Let me end with the reminder that God can handle the weight of your pain. Saying yes to a relationship with Jesus offers us opportunities to pray at any given time. It amazes me that I can talk to God anytime, anywhere, about ANYTHING. My prayers don't have to be pretty and put together. They don't have to sound high and lofty and like they belong in a church with stained glass and a cathedral ceiling. I find hope in pouring out my heart to the God of hope.

If you're new to the Bible, the book of Psalms is full of great examples of how we can run to God with all our emotions, and not just the pretty ones. Trauma can bring out all the feelings. Many of the Psalms contain a wide range of emotions in one chapter. If you're struggling to connect to God or find hope, I encourage you to take a journey of the heart by reading the prayers in Psalms. Psalms 13, Psalms 22 and Psalms 23 are great chapters to start with.

As we end this journey together, I'd love to speak a prayer of hope over you.

Dear Jesus, I pray for my very brave, very strong friend. I pray they experience your love, and that it gives them hope. I pray that you will help them as they take steps into their new normal. I pray for them to know you are with them—that you see them and have not forgotten them. I pray you provide good support people for them. That you will walk with them as they heal and have a story to tell. I pray they experience you holding the weight of their pain, struggle and story. In Jesus name, Amen.

Heart Work: Bricks, Blessings, and the Beginning of Hope

You did it. You read *Hope Beneath the Rubble*. Whether it took you ten days, ten months, or ten years—I want you to know this:

You are still standing.

You are healing.

You are creating space to hope again.

Let's take a moment to reflect on what this journey has meant for you. No pressure to have "answers," just an invitation to notice.

1. Return to the Rubble

Look back over your journey in this book. What part of your life still feels like rubble?

- What has started to rebuild?
- What feels brand new or surprising?

Write freely here:

_____

_____

_____

_____

_____

_____

2. Rebuild with What Remains

Like my youth group's mission trips *(minus the jalapeños and rusty nails)*, rebuilding sometimes means working with both new materials *and* what you already have.

- 🌿 What part of the "old you" do you want to carry into your healing journey?
- 🌿 What new tools, truths, or perspectives are you bringing forward?

3. Hope Feels Risky Sometimes

Hope doesn't always show up in grand gestures. Sometimes, it whispers. Sometimes, it wobbles. Sometimes, it sounds like, "Maybe I *could* take one next step . . . "

🌿 Finish this sentence: *Hope today looks like . . .*

_____

_____

_____

_____

_____

_____

🌿 And this one: *The risk I'm willing to take this week is . . .*

_____

_____

_____

_____

_____

_____

4. Write Your Own Nehemiah Verse

Inspired by Nehemiah 6:16, write your version below.
"So the wall was finished . . . and they knew it had been done with the help of God."

So, the healing began . . . And I knew it had been done with the help of:

_____

_____

_____

_____

_____

_____

_____

_____

_____

_____

_____

_____

_____

_____

5. Leave Yourself a Blessing

Write a note to your future self, some-thing you can come back to in a month, a year, or whenever you need a reminder that you are brave, beloved, and still rebuilding.

You are brave, beloved, and still rebuilding.

Start with:

Dear Future Me, you've come so far . . .

Celebrate this chapter (and this chapter of your life). Blow up a balloon, bake a brownie, sit under a cozy blanket with your favorite tea. You've been digging through rubble—and now you're laying the bricks of something beautiful.

ACKNOWLEDGMENTS

I'm deeply grateful to every supporter of Coming Alive Ministries whose investment has enabled me to continue traveling the world and standing with people on their holy ground of suffering to provide hope beneath the rubble.

This book was birthed out of a trip to the Dominican Republic, so I especially want to thank my Haitian sisters and Jon Jon, Morgan, Jamie, and Elizabeth, who asked me to teach on trauma. That one yes on the table led to this book.

I have the BEST family in the world, and I'm so thankful for their support. My parents are amazing and have taught me to love deep and wide. And this book would not have happened without multiple trips up the street to the Humbert house. I love being your neighbor, sister, and Aunt Nenn! Michelle, Todd, Alex, Hope, Abbi and Jacob Ray—I love you!

The team at Market Refined Media & Publishing is THE BEST, and I don't want to work on any ministry project without you. Mandy, I'm so grateful for your friendship, wisdom, and the fantastic company you've built. And Sarah Jacobson, I'm so glad I met you at the Refined Conference because this book wouldn't have happened without your coaching!

I'm deeply grateful to God for the adventures He's taken me on as I live with my yes on the table—I pray He uses this offering to bring hope and healing.

APPENDIX

It would be my great honor to continue walking with you through the rubble towards hope and healing. By accessing the QR code below, you'll find bonus guides, additional resources and teaching videos all created with you in my mind.

I'm praying for you,
my friend!

NOTES

1. *She Reads Truth Bible*, CSB (Nashville: Holman Bibles/She Reads Truth, 2017), 727.

2. "Neural Plasticity," APA Dictionary of Psychology, accessed February 28, 2024, https://dictionary.apa.org/neural-plasticity.

3. Melanie Greenberg, "Understanding the Trauma Brain," Psychology Today, June 30, 2021, accessed February 28, 2024, https://www.psychologytoday.com/us/blog/the-mindful-self-express/202106/understanding-the-trauma-brain.

4. "Neuroplasticity," Psychology Today, last modified October 2, 2019, https://www.psychologytoday.com/us/basics/neuroplasticity.

5. Blight, Wendy, *Rest for Your Soul: A Bible Study on Solitude, Silence, and Prayer*, InScribed Collection (Nashville: HarperChristian Resources, 2023), 6.

6. Shapiro, Francine and Margot Silk Forrest, *EMDR: The Breakthrough Therapy for Overcoming Anxiety, Stress and Trauma* (New York: Basic Books, 2004), 25–26.

7. Ibid., 26.

8. Kolber, Aundi. *Try Softer: A Fresh Approach to Move Us out of Anxiety, Stress, and Survival Mode—and into a Life of Connection and Joy* (Carol Stream, IL: Tyndale Momentum, 2020), 37.

9. Kolber, Aundi (@aundikolber), "Trauma happens when we experience a profound rupture in safety (related to emotions/relationships/faith/health/reality, etc.) and the repair doesn't match the wound." *Instagram*, February 26, 2024. https://www.instagram.com/p/C303JRrPlkv.

10. *APA Dictionary of Psychology*, s.v. "trigger," accessed July 28, 2025, https://dictionary.apa.org/trigger.

11. Psych Central Staff Writer, BSN, RN, "How to Identify and Overcome Trauma Triggers," *Psych Central*, November 8, 2021, https://psychcentral.com/health/trauma-triggers.

12. Mazi Robinson, *After Trauma: Hope*, video course, Jenn Hand Online Store, https://jenniferhand.org/product/after-trauma-hope-guide.

13. Cleveland Clinic, "Parasympathetic Nervous System (PSNS)," *Cleveland Clinic*, accessed August 4, 2025, https://my.clevelandclinic.org/health/body/23266-parasympathetic-nervous-system-psns#overview.

14. Smyth, Joshua M. et al., "Online Positive Affect Journaling in the Improvement of Mental Distress and Well-Being in General Medical Patients with Elevated Anxiety Symptoms: A Preliminary Randomized Controlled Trial," *JMIR Mental Health* 5, no. 4 (October 2018): e11290, https://doi.org/10.2196/11290.

15. *Elf*, directed by Jon Favreau (Burbank, CA: New Line Cinema, 2003), film.

16. Hand, Jennifer, *My Yes Is on the Table: Moving from Fear to Faith* (Chicago: Moody Publishers, 2022), 40.

ABOUT THE AUTHOR

Jennifer Hand, Executive Director of Coming Alive Ministries, and author of *My Yes is on the Table: Moving From Fear to Faith* wishes she could sit down and have a strong cup of coffee with each of you and ask you, "What makes you come alive?"

Jennifer founded Coming Alive Ministries in 2012 and loves the honor of traveling nationally and internationally, providing the invitation to come alive in Christ through conferences, retreats, written resources, and counseling.

Jennifer has had the joy of serving in over 50 countries and speaking at around 40 events a year. With her master's degree in trauma counseling, God has opened a unique door for Jennifer to respond after natural disasters around the world, providing trauma counseling and the hope of Christ on the holy ground of suffering.

Jennifer would love to keep up with you in her cozy internet corner of the world at www.jenniferhand.org or on social media @comingalivejenn or Jennifer Hand on Facebook.

www.ingramcontent.com/pod-product-compliance
Lightning Source LLC
Chambersburg PA
CBHW051203120626
46547CB00012B/1182